The Black Girl's Guide to Healing Emotional Wounds

Nijiama Smalls

Cover by Vox Illustrations

ISBN eBook: 978-1-7346928-0-8

ISBN paperback: 978-1-7346928-1-5

ISBN Hardcover: 978-1-7346928-2-2

To my husband, Shamon, I am grateful for your wisdom, selflessness, and unconditional love.

To my sister, Felicia, and all my close friends, thank you for loving me even during the times that I was unlovable.

To all my fellow Black girls that struggle just like I do and have suffered from life's hurts as I have. May God give you the grace and power to grow, learn, heal, and build a sisterhood that empowers future generations.

Contents

Introduction

Take a walk with me, and I'll introduce you to four women I know. See if you know them too.

Sara

She walks into the double glass doors of the high-rise office building in downtown Washington, DC. Her pointy black stiletto pumps tap lightly across the marble floor as she enters the elevator. You can hear her designer bag swish across the bottom of her pencil skirt as she passes through the hallway. Dressed to the nines, Sara has earned a bachelor's and master's degree from one of the nation's top historically black colleges and universities. She is well-spoken, sharp, and driven. Armed with a photographic memory, she has earned a high-paying position as a finance manager for one of the nation's largest accounting firms. Sara oversees one direct report that she has a very transactional relationship with. Continuing her stroll down the hallway, she gives each of her colleagues and her direct report a perfunctory grin as she glides into her office.

Her office is bright, spacious, and decorated with her sorority paraphernalia. As she settles in, Sara opens her laptop, sips on her coffee, and prepares for the day. Soon after, her boss walks in the door and stands by her desk.

> "Good morning, Sara, how was your weekend?" he asks. She responds in an abrupt tone, "It was great Bob, how can I help you?" Bob responds, "I want to discuss the report that you created, I have some feedback for you… Uhmmm," he pauses "I'm not trying to be harmful. Please do not see this as an attack. I simply want to help you grow within your role." She braces herself as he proceeds to provide her the feedback. "You put the wrong data in column X and you should sort by the numerator." As Bob is

talking, Sara becomes filled with anger. She is responsible for creating the report, and she believes she should be free to do that without any input from Bob. After listening, she says, "Bob I have been doing these reports for a while and I know what I'm doing. That's why you hired me. If I need your help, I will ask." Bob shakes his head and leaves her office.

Sara is a tough girl. She does not allow anyone to correct her, put her in her place or disrespect her. "I am very direct," is how she normally introduces herself to new people, letting them know upfront that she will not tolerate any level of disrespect. She says exactly what's on her mind without weighing the costs. Her colleagues deem her intimidating and unapproachable. Sara makes it clear that she is not at work to make friends or to even be friendly. She does not partake in company festivities, celebrations, or after-hours networking events, which doesn't help her change her reputation.

Sara has been eyeing the position of director of finance with her company since it was posted internally. She reads the job description daily knowing that she meets each of the criteria for the role. She has the skills, education, and abilities however, she keeps getting negative performance reviews because of her attitude and has even been written up for it. Sara is known to be difficult to work with and confrontational.

Although she enjoys the work that she does, Sara is unhappy with the company and has even turned bitter towards it. Because of her poor inter-office skills and heated confrontations, which resulted in human resources issues, she has been moved under three different managers. She has found each manager to be difficult to work with and the working relationships have ended negatively. Since she feels that she has hit a brick wall with her employer, she wants to find a position with another company however this will be the third employer she has worked for in three and a half years. She feels stuck and that's causing her a great deal of anger. The good projects and cool assignments within the company are being given to other colleagues. Her boss and her bosses' boss both seem to avoid her at all costs. She confides in one friend that tolerates her as most other colleagues seem to wish her gone as well.

Shawna

The bookstore is where you will find thirty-something Shawna. She is reserved, analytical, and enjoys reading. She doesn't enjoy the social scene, parties, or small talk, and is awkwardly quiet in social settings. Therefore, she prefers books, Netflix, and animals — she adopts and cares for rescue dogs and cats — over people. Over the years, she has had many friends — high school friends, college friends, work friends, etc. But, along the way something happens. Someone will say or do something to hurt her or they will cross a line that she has created that they may have been unaware of.

After each incident, she quiets herself, never expressing her true feelings. She spends time replaying the conversations over and over in her head, fantasizing about what she should have said and the meaning behind every word mentioned. To ease the pain, she distances herself from her offender. For Shawna, it's much easier to create distance than to courageously broach a conversation about it. Eventually, the distance becomes no contact at all.

At this point in her life, Shawna longs for solid relationships and even misses the people she's cut off but finds them taxing; they require too much work to maintain. She has grown weary and now finds it easier to remain alone and unseen. The desire for meaningful relationships doesn't go away, yet she does not know how to find a way out of the cycle that she is in.

Nefertiti

Tall, chocolate, handsome, well-spoken, and successful is the type of man that Brooklyn native Nefertiti desires. He's confident, secure, charming, tough, and charismatic, but sensitive and emotional when it comes to her. He enjoys being her provider and puts her on a pedestal because she is his queen. This the man that Nefertiti fantasizes sweeping her off her feet, similar to the characters in romantic comedies. These fantasies have been a part of Nefertiti's thoughts since she was a young girl being reared by her mother and grandmother. Eventually, her fantasies led to her dating her college sweetheart, Kyle.

She fell hard and fast for the handsome and popular Kyle. Nefertiti was quiet and flew under the radar, so she enjoyed the fact that a popular boy like Kyle paid her attention. He was a guy that she tutored in college, and soon those long nights in the library turned into romantic talks. Eventually, he proved that preparing for class assignments wasn't his thing. So, he asked her to write his papers while he spent all night partying with his frat brothers. She didn't mind. She enjoyed it because it gave him a reason to keep coming back.

Nefertiti relished every compliment he gave her, even the smallest amount of attention he paid to her.
Soon they became lovers as she snuck him into her dorm room late at night for many hours of lovemaking. She loved the fact that a guy like him was interested in her and that she is in a relationship of sorts. But as fate would have it, she got pregnant, and that changed everything. Eventually, she dropped out of college to have the baby and to focus on her family. Kyle, on the other hand, remained in college and earned his degree. The two married after he graduated and on

the night of their honeymoon, Nefertiti discovered that Kyle fathered another child while she was pregnant.

Unlike the relationships she fantasized about, however, romance with Kyle does not include dates. There are no small tokens of love and appreciation shown, and no words of affirmation given. The relationship becomes mundane quickly. Kyle spends lots of time away from home as he pursues his career and personal aspirations. Somehow, those aspirations led to him engaging in several infidelities. She forgives him each time but quietly resents Kyle, not only because of the infidelities though.

Nefertiti feels that she dropped out of college to become wife and mom to Kyle and their children, putting her life and dreams on hold while he continues to pursue his dreams. She often feels lost, lonely, without direction, and not quite sure of herself. The lack of fulfillment often overwhelms her and makes her sad and angry. She resents the fact that she has not accomplished many things in her life. There are times when she is angry with herself for marrying Kyle. However, she remains committed to Kyle, their family, and their future together.

Caroline

Free-spirited and artsy are attributes that can be used to describe Caroline. Never following the crowd or trends, Caroline is funny, resourceful, and colorful. Her style is eclectic, and her mood is ever-changing. A talented singer, she devotes her free time to performing live in the city on the weekends. But this free spirit was struck by tragedy at a very early age. When Caroline was only ten years old, her father died suddenly, leaving her mother as a widow and little Caroline to cope with life without her father.

Being a passionate person, Caroline gives her whole heart to whatever and whoever her interests are. When she meets someone that she feels a connection with, it's immediate and she is all in. Although she feels entitled to their love, the larger problem is that often, the love is unrequited. She has experienced her fair share of rejection and hurt in regards to relationships. More recently, she has spent the past few years dating and has grown tired of the relationships dissipating. Many of her relationships turn into nothing more than a few late-night texts requesting sexual favors. Her frustrations have led to her finding fault with men and the dating system.

To put an end to the pain, Caroline has decided to join the feminist sexual revolution. Good sex on her own terms has become her mantra. But sexual conquest after sexual conquest has only left her feeling empty and broken. Although she has enjoyed the intimacy, when her partner leaves in the middle of the night, she feels a sense of unhappiness, realizing she longs for more than just sexual rendezvous. She thought this new experience would make her feel in control and powerful, but instead, it makes her feel like no more than a used wash-cloth.

Since embarking on the sexual revolution, Caroline has experienced a shift in her spirit that is inexplicable. Her anxiety has increased, and she finds herself being annoyed by small things that previously would not bother her. There have also been days when she feels such heaviness within her spirit that she can't even get out of bed. Caroline continues to long for connection, but at this point, she has lost her way.

Triggered- a strong emotional reaction of fear, shock, anger, or worry, especially because you are made to remember something bad that has happened in the past. [1]

Sis, do any of these women sound like you? You might not want to admit it but let me share something with you — each of these women represent various parts of us; the parts of us that we mourn, as well as the parts that keep us up at night, crying and on our knees praying. Typically, we blame these problems on external issues — primarily saying to ourselves that it's really the fault of the other people involved. "It's all her fault or his fault," we tell ourselves. The reality is that we share a large part of the blame. These situations are triggers that are pointing us towards bigger issues. They are surface issues that reflect greater internal conflicts that have not been specifically dealt with — these conflicts are better known as unhealed emotional wounds.

Trauma can be defined as a psychological, emotional response to an event or an experience that is deeply distressing or disturbing. This trauma definition can refer to something upsetting, such as being involved in an accident, having an illness or injury, losing a loved one, or going through a divorce. However, it can also encompass the far extreme and include experiences that are severely damaging, such as rape or torture.[4]

If left untreated, the trauma does not go away, instead, it will manifest itself into unhealed emotional wounds that alter our behaviors and perceptions. They change us from being the people we are meant to be. They can cause a sweet, kind, harmless person to display vile and evil behavior when triggered. Unhealed emotional wounds can cause a person to feel inferior and deeply insecure. They can cause an otherwise smart person to make foolish choices that result in further emotional harm.

How many times have you heard a black girl say, "I don't trust women", "I don't get along with other women", "I hate my boss" (well that's one that we all say) or what about "I won't let anyone get over on me", "I don't like working for a black woman", or "all men are dogs"? Perhaps you have even said these things yourself, Lord knows I have. These thoughts come from a person that has become jaded by an unhealed wound. Wounds change our perception and cause us to needlessly suffer. I often say that by the time a person becomes 30yrs old, they have experienced at least one major break up, friendship betrayal, personal or professional setbacks, rejection, and many transitions. Depending on the meaning that we assign to these situations, they can cause us to become emotionally ill; anything that triggers that hurt can cause us to react negatively. We need to end the suffering and get out of our own way so that we can continue to develop meaningful relationships across the board, the most important relationship being the one we have with ourselves.

According to Census data, on average, black women were paid 61 percent of what non-Hispanic white men were paid in 2017. That means it takes the typical black woman 19 months to earn what the average white man earns in 12 months. That's even worse than the national earnings ratio for all women, 80 percent, as reported in AAUW's *The Simple Truth about the Gender Pay Gap*. This gap persists even though black women participate in the workforce at much higher rates than most other women. [2]

Why did I give you those statistics you ask? Well, we all know that racism and sexism have a lot to do with these statistics, but we can control this to some degree by mobilizing ourselves and using the powers we obtain to love and support other black girls. We need to create a palpable sisterhood in which we share resources amongst each other instead of keeping them quiet. We need to be willing to embrace our sisters instead of excluding them and support our sisters instead of shading them. But, it all starts with healing our emotional wounds so that we can change the way we see each other. We should be viewing each other as sisters instead of competitors. We should owe each other compassion instead of critique, and honor instead of side-eyes. Why? Because it's necessary to help heal our own and our sister's emotional wounds.

We spend our lives fighting battles that are not meant to be fought; they need to be healed. Unhealed emotional wounds do not go away if left untreated. They may hide for a bit, but trust me, they will resurface when triggered and can even grow bigger. These wounds will keep us bound until we deal with them. They can prevent us from being the best friend, daughter, mother, spouse, leader, employee, and entrepreneur that we can be. These wounds resurface over and over in various situations causing us pain and suffering. We are doomed to repeat the same situations and will be stuck in a vicious toxic cycle until we deal and heal.

These unhealed wounds also steal from us — they take away our happiness, joy, and peace. How many times have you had an argument with your significant other, parent, family member, or friend that kept you awake at night? How many times have you made a choice that bothered your soul? How many times have you lost a relationship with a friend, co-worker, or family member and it deeply hurt you? How many times have you lost an opportunity, got fired, or had to leave from your job as a result of your attitude or behavior? These are your emotional wounds speaking to you. They are crying out for healing.

I have had my share of cavities in my lifetime. I have a sweet tooth, so I eat lots of sweet foods — I'm working on improving that habit. If you have ever had a cavity, you know the enormous amount of pain they can cause. Many times, with cavities, it's not just the tooth that is in pain, it's the gum and the entire side of the mouth where the tooth is located that will ache. For me, having a cavity causes enough pain that it interrupts my daily life.

Many times, I have tried to ignore the pain from the cavity, unfortunately, it only gets worse and if you allow it to linger, infection will set in which will cause further damage. I have also tried to use over-the-counter medication on the cavity with the hope that it will go away, but it only worked for a short time. The medicine simply masks the pain until it wears off. The tooth must be treated properly; the decay must be removed, and a filling must be placed in the area where the decay is so that the tooth can heal properly and you can enjoy life without pain. It's the same with our emotional wounds. We must pay attention to the triggers that point us to our wounds then treat the wounds with the right techniques to allow them to heal properly. The negativity must be removed and replaced with positive techniques so that we can heal and not cause ourselves or others anymore suffering.

The following list includes some of the most common emotional triggers, meaning we react when we feel as though we aren't getting or will not get one of these things that are very important to us.

Acceptance	Respect	Be Liked
Be Understood	Be Needed	Be Valued
Be in Control	Be Right	Be Treated Fairly
Attention	Comfort	Freedom
Peacefulness	Balance	Consistency
Order	Variety	Love
Safety	Predictability	Included
Fun	New Challenges	Autonomy[3]

Sara, Shawna, Nefertiti, and Caroline are great examples of how we battle emotional triggers caused by unhealed trauma. These wounds are stealing their peace while causing them to get in their own way.

Healing emotional wounds is a process. They do not heal overnight. It requires lots of time, patience and hard work but let me tell ya', this soul work is worth it. However, it's going to hurt like hell before it's going to get better.

Trust me, I'm not writing this book to be judgmental. I've spent many years in therapy (I'm always on somebody's couch), and many nights in my prayer closet. I've conducted lots of research and lots of soul-searching. I am certainly not trying to paint my black sisters negatively. However, I think it's important that we be honest with ourselves so that we can heal. One thing I have realized: this soul work is more than worth it. The freedom and peace that I now know is invaluable. And the healthy relationships that I have developed are priceless.

In this journey, you are going to peel back all the layers that got you to this place. As you journal the answers to the questions at the end of the chapters (I recommend doing this in your quiet time or with a solid group of girl-friends that you do life with), take as much time as necessary to self-reflect and to be completely honest with yourself; and you must pray as you are reading this book and ask for God's guidance and support. The honesty is going to be devastating at times because this journey requires you to take the band-aids off the wounds and confront them head-on.

The good news is, this will be the last time these issues will hold you back. Your hurts and wounds will no longer define you. You are going to be free to love and healthily receive love. You are getting ready to be emotionally free! Ask yourself, are you ready to experience freedom? Are you ready to love? Are you ready to stop hurting and being hurt? It's your time to live the rest of your life in total emotional freedom! Let's go!

Questions to Journal

Which of the women described do you feel you identify with? How? *Shawna*

What would you like to gain from reading this book?

• Learning how to be comfortable being myself. Accepting my feeling. Processing my feelings. Not judging myself and others negatively.

~~Elubb~~ "'s your coming along honey, I really believe it will help to expand on these things

Chapter 1

How Did We Get Here?

Generational Trauma

Let's face it, many of us walking on this planet are suffering from emotional trauma and unhealed emotional wounds. The pain, betrayal, and suffering from years past continue to haunt us emotionally to this day. What is important to note is that black girls suffer differently than our sisters from other cultures, and the trauma stems from vastly different origins.

As black girls, it's critical for us to understand our trauma and live in our truth so that we can deal and heal properly. I chose to focus this book on black girls because I feel we have so many roadblocks to our healing; the secrets we keep in our families, the stigma of mental health and mental health services within our community, the lack of communication during our early development, and the lack of healthy conflict resolution skills — these factors foster an environment that allows black girls to suffer. We have had to learn, on our own, how to cope with the blows that life deals us and that has caused us to develop bad habits and unhealthy coping skills that we have passed down from one generation to the next.

Many signs show us that you or your fellow black girl is suffering. Within the Black community, we have normalized and even celebrated behaviors that indicate unhealed emotional wounds. Not only have we normalized these behaviors but we have nurtured them and made some of them part of our culture.

Here are a few signs that indicate unhealed emotional trauma:

- Inability to celebrate the success of others
- Believe the worst of someone's intentions
- Defensiveness
- Throwing shade
- Holding grudges
- One-upping
- Cynicism
- Inability to trust
- Mood swings
- Selfishness
- Financial irresponsibility
- Extreme sensitivity
- Bragging
- Short temper
- Lack of self-control
- People pleasing
- Lying, uncontrollable lying

Let's be completely honest with ourselves, how many times have you walked through life with an attitude like, "if you say one thing wrong to me, I will quickly gather you?" If not, I'm sure you can name a few black girls that have that attitude. Some of that stems from the way we have been conditioned, but, some of it is unhealed trauma speaking.

One of the main staple dishes within the black community is potato salad. You can find this dish at almost any Sunday dinner or Thanksgiving meal. In the summer, across the country, potato salads make their way to various picnics, cook-outs, and spades gatherings. The truth is, potato salad is not an easy dish to make. Usually, the auntie or neighbor that can make the delicious potato salad is called upon to make it and is typically deemed the queen of the event because of her potato salad making abilities. At each event, you will hear soft whispers asking, "who made the potato salad?" so that people will know whether to indulge or steer clear.

I've tried making potato salad several times and each time it was an epic fail. There are several factors that impact potato salad — the way the potatoes are cooked, and the type and amount of ingredients put into it. If you cook the potatoes for too long, it will make the dish too soggy. If you do not cook them long enough, it makes the potatoes hard and crunchy and no one likes that. Needless to say, I'm never asked to bring potato salad to events. In the black community, you only get one chance to make a bad batch of potato salad and if you do show up with janky potato salad it will be frowned upon. Your potato salad will never be invited back to the event. And if you dare show up to an event with your not-up-to par potato salad, it will be tossed to the side or placed in the bottom of a deep freezer where no one will ever find it.

Like potato salad, life starts out as simple as potatoes sitting on a shelf ripe and ready to be converted to what the cook wants them to be — in this case potato salad. But during that process, things occur to change our state and that impacts how we turn out or show up. And sadly, how we show up, determines how we are treated. We need to be careful of how we are showing up and do the work to assure we are showing up as our true authentic selves, ready to love and to be loved.

Let's dig deeper into how we are showing up: Years ago, I was a wedding planner. I literally planned hundreds of weddings across the Washington, DC area and most of my clients were women of color. It was not as glamorous of a job as movies depict. There were many long hours and late nights, and a loss of my weekend social life. There were also many times that I had to carry heavy equipment up and down long hallways and steep staircases in various venues. Then, of course, there was the occasional bridezilla that I had to encounter. What was worse than the bridezilla was their family and friends. I have dealt with many mean girls and many mean mothers and best friends. There were times when I felt like a piece of raw steak in a den filled with lions. Can I be honest with y'all? I had reached the point where I did not want to plan weddings that involved black girls. That's right, I did not want to help my own race with the most important day of their life.

I remember planning a wedding for a dear, sweet bride. She knew what she wanted and had planned the bulk of the event on her own. She simply needed me to tie up the loose ends and coordinate on the big day. I had a bridal package for that and it was fine with me.

The wedding was probably the most difficult that I have ever planned. Not because of the bride, the vendors, or the logistics but because of everything else — mainly the bridal party. Within the wedding party, there were three hostesses and six bridesmaids. These girls were a nightmare to work with. They complained about the dresses, the costs, the location of the rehearsal dinner and the shoes. They showed up late to rehearsal and refused to follow the poor bride's choices. What a nightmare!

Not only did they give the bride a hard time, but they also chose to take an issue with me as the wedding planner for some reason. As soon as I walked into the room and introduced myself, I was faced with a bunch of dry hellos and rolled eyes.

During that entire event, every time someone asked them to do something, they flat out refused. Every tiny detail that was missed, they were quick to point it out. They chuckled as we practiced four times to assure the bride was comfortable. They laughed and said, "where did she come from? I guess anybody can be a coordinator now" when the Pastor and I had differences in opinions on the order of ceremonies. Even more, they were aggressive and confrontational with anyone that tried to give them direction. They even managed to pull other people into it; Oh, they had a ball. These women name-called and celebrated every small failure and rolled their eyes when the actual wedding was perfect. When asked to do their parts, they flat out refused. At the end of it all, I was surprised and hurt for myself and the bride. Now, these were not the only black girls that I have encountered that behaved like this.

The irony in all of this was I should not have been hurt. I have also been the one that sized up another black woman when she walked into the room. I check out her hair, clothes, shoes, and then decide how I'm going to respond to her. There have also been times when a woman has been in power or doing something that I have wanted to do, I placed her under heavy scrutiny. "How did she get this role?" Demeaning her experience and education, doubting her qualifications. Panting as I wait for the tea or dirt on her. And anyone that could produce some of her past failures was the winner in my book.

But the question is how did we get here? When faced with a situation such as this, why do we choose to play the mean girl instead of being loving and kind? Why do we choose to watch someone suffer (and oftentimes enjoy it) rather than pick up someone that may be falling and help them succeed? Why do we make these bad choices?

To answer this question, we must venture back into the evil days of slavery. What is often left out of historical discussions regarding slavery is the wounds and trauma that black women gained during slavery. The viciousness of plantation life pit women against women as they were compared to each other and auctioned off to the highest bidder. These women were then selected to be in the field or the house based on complexion, physique, age, and/or talents. Imagine having to do back-breaking labor for long hours of the day outside while the blazing hot sun scorches your back day after day. As you toil in the sun, you see the other women, the women that should be considered your sisters, working inside of the much cooler house. We all know that working inside of the house had its own set of problems but the sting here is that your quality of life and value is determined by someone that deemed you too dark, not easy enough on the eyes, or less appealing in some other way.

To take it a step further, also imagine watching white women relax all day and enjoy the freedoms that you can't even fathom because your skin color is deemed not good enough. You labor hard all day as they socialize, plan events, love on their children and families while your children are ripped from your arms and taught to labor instead of playing and being educated. You watch as your husband is abused, berated, demeaned, and belittled all day without the ability to stand up for his family or himself. You and your loved ones are treated as disposable beings that bear limited value instead of beautiful souls. Now that's traumatic.

Soon, black woman that served on the plantation eventually realized that to get out of the miserable circumstances and to make the situation better, we needed to mobilize and be better and that sometimes meant being better than our sisters. We needed to perform better, look better, and/or serve better. When your quality of life is threatened, you rely on desperation to find a solution. And desperate people do desperate things. Thus, the competition, distrust, and resentment took formation. It is my belief that this is the point where many women in our culture began to see each other as competitors rather than allies.

It did not stop there. During reconstruction and the civil rights era, the divide between black women still existed. There was still lots of talk within the black community about colorism, physique, facial features, and hair texture. The tools that were used by oppressors to keep us bound, miserable, and enslaved had become indoctrinated and even embraced within our community. This is toxic y'all. During those days, if you wanted to make someone angry, you called them black, blacky, darky, nappy-head, and bald-head (if a black woman's hair was not considered long enough). If a black person's features were not deemed European enough, they were made fun of. Your nose could not appear too big or too wide and your lips could not be too full.

Now during that time, some men began to fantasize and desire what they felt they could not have and that was a white woman. She was considered the prize. If they could not have her they wanted something close- a light-skinned woman. There were many light-skinned women during that time because of the racial fraternizing between Indian slaves and African slaves on the plantations along with slave rape which resulted in many racially mixed women. These were black women with fair skin and long straight or curly hair. They often had European features- thin lips, skinny noses, etc. And these women often became the object of the affection of many black men. We have always heard of many women across races, in general, describing their ideal man as, "tall, dark and handsome." That description is never made for women, "tall, dark, and beautiful."

Lighter-skinned women with European features were often placed on pedestals and they became the standard of beauty. They were singled out and given names- redbone, high yellow, etc. And our lighter-skinned sisters felt resentment and reacted to it. This changed us from viewing each other as sisters but as a threat at times. Let's be honest, how many times have you sized up another woman that walked into a room and thought "who is she?", "she thinks she is something special." Ladies, this is where some of that thinking was birthed.

The resentment towards darker-skinned women and the elevation of status of the light-skinned women made the animosity between women of color even deeper. Women were being left out of social circles and obtaining certain positions because of colorism. It hit our community like a plague and sadly- it still exists.

And that, my sisters, is the atmosphere that our great grandmothers and grandmothers were born into. That environment made it easy to look upon another woman with envy and jealousy. These behaviors are a direct result of our generational trauma and unhealed wounds. Trauma has the ability to change our DNA. In the *Scientific American*, Erika Beras reports, "trauma can be passed down to offspring due to epigenetic changes in DNA. But positive experiences seem able to correct that. " [1] Not only did it change our DNA, but this environment also made it hard for women to fully grasp the concept of self- love, and acceptance. Our ancestors suffered tremendously and therefore we suffer to some degree.

Not only have we passed down our generational trauma, but we have embraced it and made it a part of our culture; In the 70s, Betty Wright sang about the "Clean Up Woman".[2] In the 80s, Salt and Peppa rapped, "I'll Take Your Man."[3] In the 90s Brandy and Monica dueled in the song, "The Boy is Mine",[4] and today Cardi B says, "I Give Broads Chills."[5] Do you see how the competition amongst black girls has been not only perpetuated but fully embraced by our community?

"I've seen his car at the girl's house that lives on Carson Drive," these are the words my mother spoke to me about a guy that I was seriously involved with in my early twenties. Rumors had been swirling around my very small yet humble town of my boyfriend's cheating. My mangled emotions and unhealed trauma would not allow me to believe it and so I continued to date him. I could not fathom the thought of him cheating and didn't even understand how he could possibly find the time to do so. I was even angry with my family for delivering the news to me. But as fate would have it, I soon discovered that he was in fact cheating with the girl on Carson Drive.

I confronted him about the cheating. After a bunch of arguing and apologies that led to his good behavior for a limited time,

I forgave him and we continued dating. What remained constant was that I was furious with the other woman. She was a woman that I did not know very well and had only seen a few times around town. Looking back on that situation, I realized how insane it was that I continued to love him while remaining woefully committed to our relationship, but I was still very much so angry with the other woman.

That year, I put all of my energy into hating her. When I saw her, I made a point to single her out to all of my friends that she should not be trusted and that "we," collectively, hated her. My friends obliged and tapped into their unhealed wounds and hated this woman that they did not know that had caused them no harm. I spread rumors around town that she was a trick, a whore, a slut, a THOT, and an overall bad person. If I saw her, I made it a point to roll my eyes and let her know that I hated her. I wanted nothing good for this woman. She was my enemy. For some reason, it was easy for me to hate her and a challenge for me to hold him accountable for his infidelities. After all, he was the one that had all the information and had made the commitment to me. What I did not realize was that I was acting out on the generational trauma that plagued my family.

This behavior that I displayed, I have witnessed in my grandmother, and mother, and I'm sure that if I dug deep enough, I would see it further down through my lineage. This had become my family's way of handling trauma of this sort. I continued to carry the grief of my ancestors and that truly shaped my attitude and behavior towards women.

Questions to Journal

Which of the signs of unhealed trauma do you display? What causes you to do so?

How do you respond when you are offended? What causes you to respond the way you do?

Have you ever responded negatively to a black girl that you have come in contact with? What caused you to do so?

How has colorism impacted your life?

How have you felt about your lover's previous partners or your ex-lover's current partners?

Family Secrets

Ladies, our ancestors suffered immensely, and their suffering became our family secrets. Secrets are those traumatic situations that we keep to ourselves because of shame. Those secrets that our families do not discuss keep us stuck in cycles of pain. Show me a family that has a lot of drama and, I will bet you there are some secrets that are bottled up that have passed down generational hurts. I believe our ancestors are crying out from the grave screaming for us to expose those nasty family secrets that continue to haunt us. For this reason, I believe that it is highly important that our families move away from secrets.

Trust me, I have many secrets in my family. We keep secrets because we feel they hide our pain or to protect our loved ones. Some secrets are just too difficult to even talk about. But the secrets do not cover up the hurt, instead, they keep us bound and enslaved to them. Keeping a secret never protects anyone except the perpetrator, when one is present, and it also causes harm to the innocent.

My grandfather married my grandmother when they were teens in the early 1950s. My grandmother later discovered that he was a closeted gay man. Today, in many parts of our country, when someone shares they are gay, it's as if they are saying they are wearing a blue shirt — it's just another Tuesday and people go on about their business. During those earlier times in our country's history, however, it was thought of as the worst thing a black man living in the Deep South could possibly do.

This was the unspoken secret in my family, no one dared to mention it. The secret in and of itself caused lots of pain in my family. My mother, who, as a child, was left in the care of her father while her mother was masking her trauma with an affair, witnessed my grandfather having sex with another man in the next room. She was never given the ability to speak of it in a healthy way. Therefore, she kept it bottled up. There is much harm that we cause ourselves when we keep things bottled up. When severe emotional trauma occurs during our formative years, our development is stunted at the age the trauma occurs. Therefore, for many years, my mother became stuck in an arrested development that she could not break away from.

We kept this situation completely hidden and never discussed it because of one primary factor — shame (the aching feeling of humiliation). It is damaging. Shame causes us to feel inferior and hypervigilant. It also causes us to behave defensively. And because of the shame, my entire family suffered — my grandmother suffered her entire life from the betrayal and the act of living a lie to keep up appearances and my grandfather suffered from the secret in and of itself, which caused him to suffer years of guilt. My mom and uncles suffered from growing up in a home with lots of tension and strife. And most of the grandchildren suffered by not having whole parents, but never truly acknowledging the source. The shame and guilt of that secret resulted in lots of dysfunction, conflict, and bitterness that was passed down through my family. Even to this day, there is still blame thrown around, which are truly just immature emotional reactions to triggers. The pain of that secret keeps our family stuck in a cycle of bitterness that we have a hard time breaking away from. This secret is the hardest thing for my family to discuss, but the thing that everyone thinks about and the thing that impacts us the most.

This secret was just the start of our entire family burying their secrets in the depths of their psyche. And because our family has a pattern of harbouring secrets, it has also created an environment in which we cannot resolve conflicts because we do not understand the benefits of open, honest communication. In fact, it is frowned upon in my family. Therefore, when we are hurt or have an issue, we bottle it up until we explode. Many of our hurts surface during large family functions. That is typically the time that one of us says something that triggers another family member causing that person to emotionally explode. After the blow-up, they give each other the silent treatment for a while until they feel they are "over it". This is a very toxic pattern that stems from secrets.

Secrets can and will control our lives and determine our future. Because we keep issues hidden, future generations will never understand what they will have to battle against or why they behave the way they do or make the choices they make. That's how the cycles keep repeating. We need to embrace an atmosphere of open and honest communication within our families so that we can uncover the unhealed wounds and generational traumas that plague us. I have always believed that part of our family reunions should be healing sessions which include a time for the older generations to share, break down the family trauma, and identify outlets that help the family heal as a unit. I find it perplexing that our older generations choose to hold on to secrets instead of sharing them with the objective of healing. Now that is how we truly leave a legacy — a legacy of healing, a legacy of breaking vicious cycles. Truth is painful, and it hurts to face it, but we continue to suffer when we try to mask it. Open communication is necessary to prevent future generations from being carriers of trauma.

In the Bible, John 8:32 says, "and you will know the truth and the truth will set you free."[1] You will never experience true freedom if you continue to worry about being judged by other flawed humans and that fear is one of the primary reasons people keep secrets. Please hear this: you will never heal if you carry shame and guilt in your heart. You will always be easily triggered, guarded, easily hurt and over-reactive.

I have met many black women that suffer from anxiety and symptoms of anxiety, including myself. This is another malady, like insomnia, that can be linked to generational trauma. When I look back through my familial history, I notice that my grandmother suffered from symptoms similar to those of anxiety. I also notice currently that my mother still suffers as well. I believe our anxiety is caused by the way we handle conflict or traumatic events. It is also caused by trauma that has changed our DNA. We have not learned to implement good coping skills and to use communication to heal. Therefore, we are easily stressed or triggered when something goes wrong which leads to anxiety. We cover up the symptoms with medication, but the trauma also needs to be healed through communication and therapy.

Questions to Journal

How close is your family? What prohibits your family from being close?

What secrets does your family keep?

How do these secrets impact your family today?

How do the secrets impact you?

What negative patterns or cycles have you noticed within your family?

How can you heal and help your family heal?

Mommy Issues

"My mother's overbearing personality made it hard to think for myself and form my own opinions. During my adolescent and young adult years, instead of discovering who I was, I constantly had my mother telling me who I should be, what I should wear, what I should do as a profession, and who I should date. Now as an adult, I'm having to do the work of self- discovery which should have taken place years ago."
Kennedy J.

Our very first relationship is with our mothers. Our moms teach us what unconditional love looks like and paints the very first picture of woman to woman relationships. For many of us, our moms grew up in the 50s, 60s, 70s, and early 80s. Those days were drastically different from the times we currently live in. There were no cell phones or Google, and kids could run free all day long, at least until the street light came on. Another key difference is that these were times when oppression was still prevalent, and racism was still very much alive and well. Many of our mothers were poor or lower middle class or maybe just on the cusp of middle class.

The middle class, within the black community, did not look the way it does today. There were not many fancy family trips abroad and over the top family dinners at the local five-star restaurant. Black families rarely had nannies and housekeepers during those times. Many families deemed middle class were living paycheck to paycheck. Poverty has an impact on the way a person views the world and the way they parent. The focus, during those times, was on surviving and not thriving. In contrast, many mothers in my circle today discuss school options for their children, plan play dates and vacations, and finding the right summer or after school program for their child. Those conversations between black mothers were few and far between in those days. Keeping food on the table and preventing their daughter from being "fast" and getting pregnant was the objective. Survival was the focus.

Many moms, during those days, worked long hours or two jobs for survival. There was no time for big hugs; long intimate mom to daughter talks; or words of affirmation. There was no time for them to study their children to understand their interests, see what their learning styles were and what they were curious about. There was no time to concern themselves with the development of the whole child and to affirm and appreciate their development at every stage. Therefore, many identities were not established. As children, we were left to figure it out on our own. Not having a clear picture of who you are can be damaging. If you do not know who you are, you can be doomed for a lifetime of confusion, bad decision-making, and suffering.

I once heard Bishop TD Jakes, the Pastor of the Potter's House, speak at a new year's revival service. During his speech, I heard him say something that I found to be rather profound. He mentioned in his sermon that while he was a small child riding in the car with his grandmother, she turned to him and said, "you are going to be a great man someday."[1] It surprised me that almost 50+ years later, he remembers that conversation. I can barely remember what I ate for lunch, so I was certainly shocked that he remembered something that happened so long ago. But, what it also said to me is that his grandmother studied him enough to know that he had greatness within him and that within him lied the qualities of a great man. And by her speaking those words, it gave him enough self-confidence to do just that.

Jakes was not born into wealth and he certainly did not descend from a generation of great leaders. In fact, he was born into a working-class family in the hills of West Virginia. Jakes' father died when he was ten years old of kidney failure. As a young boy, he and his mother had to care for his father before his untimely death. Yet, today he has planted one of the largest churches in the country, written numerous books, directed films, and hosted conferences that can fill up a stadium with its attendance [2] — all because someone believed in him. Because someone studied him, affirmed him, and took the time to have a conversation with him to build his self-confidence, which ultimately led him to gain the ability to become a success. Do you now see the power of establishing a child's identity through your words?

Parenting from that generation also meant they had to be tough on us. They wanted the best for us, to keep us safe and free from bad choices. So, for them, it meant yelling, harsh punishments, and strict rules. Something as minor as wearing the wrong coat to school could mean a very stiff consequence. There was always a threat of serious punishments. I can recall as a child, I received more threats than I received hugs.

They were very direct and always giving us warnings, particularly about our female friends, "don't trust her," they said, "she's not your friend." "You shouldn't have a lot of female friends." "Don't hang around those fast girls." These types of comments send messages to impressionable minds about other women — that we should not trust them, that they do not have our best interests at heart, and that young black women are hyper-sexual.

At the same time, what was just as damaging was the comparisons. Some of our mothers compared us to our family and close friends — statements like "Cousin Angie wears pretty dresses, why don't you?" "I hear our neighbor Janet is great at playing the piano, why can't you do that?"

"Joanne made all As on her report card." "Karen keeps her clothes cleaned while she plays." For a child, these internalized messages get translated to mean, I'm not as good as Karen, Cousin Angie, Janet, or Joanne. This taught us to look at the accomplishments of others and compare them to our own. This tool was used in hopes of changing our behavior. As an adult, I've learned that it was certainly not the best method because it causes so much inner conflict and turmoil that can last a lifetime. Instead of being happy for that person we were compared to, we then become envious or jealous, resentful even, "what makes her better?" We think to ourselves and are delighted when negative things happen to them that knock them off their pedestal.

Those types of comparisons can cause a child to question their parents' level of unconditional love for them. Now I'm sure that the parents that did this meant no harm and their intentions were not to hurt but to help. But imagine if the message had been, "I love you as you are" or for the child that isn't as gifted in the piano as Janet, they were studied to see what other areas they are gifted in and constantly reminded that they are talented but just in different areas. Imagine how different things would be if that had been the message.

Particularly, during that time children were told to be seen and not heard. I can recall many times when my mother or grandmother asked me to be quiet when I wanted to ask a question or make a statement in front of a group of their adult peers. My opinions were rarely asked for. Over time, I began to feel small and unseen and as if my opinion didn't matter. And that feeling doesn't go away on its own. I know many women today that struggle with feelings of inferiority and lack of self-confidence that stem from this.

Instead of having the ability to express ourselves as adults, we learned internal processing. When we internalize situations, it leads us to overthink. Overthinking has been proven to have a direct link to anxiety and depression. In the previous example of Shawna, she spent lots of time overthinking and living inside of her head which destroyed her friendships. She never felt seen as a child which caused her lots of anxiety and even led her to depression.

This idea of children being seen and not heard also meant that lots of questions from children went unasked and lots of meaningful conversations were never had. Healthy conversations about our female bodies, sex, and dating just wasn't on the "discussion table" at that time. Aside from being told not to engage in sex and not to get pregnant, that was the extent of conversations about sexuality and dating. So, once again, we were left to figure it out on our own and that was damaging. I've met many people that began viewing pornography and experimenting sexually very early on simply because they were curious, but without knowing how traumatizing those things can be.

 For those of us that recognize that some of these things were missed in our rearing, we can easily build up a silent but deadly resentment towards our mothers and that resentment can manifest itself into our relationships with authority. The way that we relate to authority figures is a reflection of our relationship with our parents.

As an example, when I first began working in a professional environment, I despised taking direction. Anyone that tried to tell me what to do, I immediately viewed them as challenging me. Whatever I was asked to do, I would argue to do the opposite and try to get them to understand why my way was better. I said whatever I wanted to anyone within the office regardless of their feelings. Similar to Sara, as we read above, I considered myself to be bold and direct and I liked the idea that people were intimidated by me. I behaved this way because I grew up with such an overbearing mother that it caused me to resent her parenting style, and I resented anyone that I assumed was trying to relate to me in that way.

I needed to feel in control at all times and could not stand for anyone to tell me what to do. The resentment I had towards my mom for her parenting style was, in many ways, causing me to behave just like her. Girl, that's how unhealed trauma grows- it causes us to behave in the same manner as the one that hurt us and that is how the cycle keeps repeating itself.

Now let's take a minute and look at our relationships with other women. There is a scene in the movie *Friday* in which Craig's mother is getting into the car and greets the younger, attractive, yet scantily clad dressed Mrs. Parker that lives across the street. She says in a low voice so that Mrs. Parker can't hear her, "Look at her. She ought to be ashamed of herself coming out here looking like that." Then she waves and says, "Hey girl." Mrs. Parker yells back, "Call me later." Then, Craig's mom replies with, "okay," [3] with a hint of annoyance to let the viewers know that she really does not like Mrs. Parker. This is a perfect example of the sometimes catty relationships we develop with other women. It is also a great example of the shade a black mom can throw. Now, women of other races I'm sure throw their share of shade. We don't have a monopoly on shade, but ours is different (Whew Chile) more upfront and in your face.

How many times have we heard our mothers, aunties, and friends of the family come together to sip tea or drink a bottle and gossip about the neighbor or whoever was the hot topic at that time? How many times have we heard the older women that raised us spend hours on the telephone gossiping to girlfriends? Yet, we have also seen them smile and chat with the person they gossiped about as if they said nothing negative at all. Gossip is a big part of every culture. I have learned to hate it because it makes us reluctant to share and be vulnerable with one another. The fear of judging and spreading rumors keeps us bound in our trauma because we do not trust what should be our safe spaces to share.

In contrast, all of us did not grow up with moms that baked cookies, checked our homework, made dinner every night, and read books to us before bed. We cannot deny that many of our mothers suffered from things that controlled their lives and choices. I am referring to things that were bigger than them, that took their focus. Whether that thing was a mental health issue, a religion, an addiction, a career, or even a lover, we knew we were not the priority.

Because our mothers were not as present as we would have liked, we had to figure it out on our own. As children, we look to our mothers to be our primary nurturers; to teach us about life and womanhood while providing protection and emotional support. When mom is unable to fulfill that role, and we do not have someone else to step in, there may be some life skills left unacquired. It also leaves a scar that is hard to bear, and the damage is hard to heal. The desire for a mother's love never deserts us, yet it leaves us hungry for a mother figure or just someone to love us the way a mother should. It also makes it hard for us to fully trust and, our relationships with other women become complicated.

Questions to Journal

Describe your mother's parenting style? How does her parenting style impact you today?

Do you trust other women?

How have you thrown shade in the past? How did you want that person to feel?

Think about the last disagreement you had with another black girl; what was the cause? How was it resolved?

Daddy Issues

"Growing up without my biological father, there was always a feeling of rejection, like I wasn't good enough for him. I know this is false, but I believe this was an internal motor for me being an overachiever for so many years. To be impressive. To impress." Tanya L.

I can remember when I was in my twenties and dating a guy that I really liked. Throughout the relationship, I displayed all the typical insecure girl behavior — checking his phone, questioning his whereabouts, assuming that he was sleeping with every single girl he was in contact with. I could not trust him because I did not have an overall trust in men, in general. I believed all the nonsense that my mom and her friends told me about men — they are no good, they are all dogs, they can't be trusted, etc. When we tell black girls this, we are damaging them instead of protecting them. And for me, the proof I had was my daddy. He wasn't present in my life, so it was easy for me to believe what they fed me. These issues manifested themselves in the very early years of my marriage. Although I married a great man, I found it difficult to trust him and my lack of trust caused me to play the insecure girl although he gave me no reason to behave that way.

Daddies play a unique yet different role in the family structure. Their rough play teaches us to take risks, their role teaches us how to lead and what masculinity and sometimes hard work looks like. Often their presence makes us feel safe and secure. Their words and affirmation have power over us. When I tell my seven-year-old daughter to go to bed she adheres yet often reluctantly at her own pace. When my husband, her father tells her to go to bed she hops up quickly to do so without question. Their words and authority are powerful and teach us to respect authority early on. When they speak, it means to take action now.

In contrast, my daughter has an adoration for her father. Her little heart melts and jumps for joy when she sees him. She also shows great concern for him. When he is sick, she wants to make sure he is fine. When he goes to work, she wants to go with him. If he could carry her in his pocket and take her with him everywhere he went she would be happy about that.

Please know that there is a difference between having a present father than having an involved father. Many women grew up with fathers that are present in the home. An involved father is not only present, but he establishes a relationship with his child very early on. He models godly character and demonstrates unconditional love. A solid father-daughter bond consists of lots of communication and spending quality time alone, just the two. A solid father-daughter bond also means that there is trust.

When fathers are not involved, if we do not have any other solid relationships to glean from, we will have a false sense and understanding of what committed relationships look like. For my family, we had very few married couples that were in loving relationships that I could look to as role models. So, I used media such as TV and movie characters to determine what a healthy marriage should be. Because of that, I thought that marriage would produce everyday happiness. Boy, was I in for a big surprise when I got married. I had no clue how much compromise and sacrifice was involved. I had to learn the hard way that marriage isn't some magic spell that produces a happily ever after effect but instead, it involves a series of choices that one has to make every single day. I also realized that I needed to deprogram some of my toxic thinking to make it work.

Very few men in my family were faithful and remained true to their wives. Growing up, I rarely saw men in my family honor and love on their wives. I did not see them take their wives out on dates, sit with them on the sofa cuddling, or compliment their new hairstyle. Also, the women in my family drilled it in my head that men were no good. I accepted that and it became my reality. I believed that men would cheat and would not treat me with the highest level of respect because that's what I had seen and heard. And sadly, that's what I attracted during my early dating experiences. It was not until I ran upon this verse:

(Jeremiah 29:11)
For I know the plans I have for you," declares the LORD, "plans to prosper you and not to harm you, plans to give you hope and a future."[1]

When I read that passage of scripture, I realized that dating unloving and unkind men was not God's plan for my life. God's thoughts towards me were positive and good and not the harm that I kept subjecting myself to. He wanted better for me but the problem was that I didn't want better for myself because I did not believe I would attract anything better. I had accepted garbage because I had been programmed to accept garbage. When I read that verse, I knew the way I was being treated by the guys that I was dating was against God's purpose for my life. I realized then that it was far better for me to be alone and whole than with a dude that didn't respect me and left me broken.

To take things a step further, since my father was not in my life, I did not have a true understanding of what men actually needed from a woman in a relationship. Goodness, during that time, dating me was tough, almost a nightmare because I did not understand how men needed to be loved. I was clueless to the fact that men equated respect with love. So, I spent many times blatantly disrespecting my boyfriends and not fully understanding why they would be upset about it. "Get over it," I thought. It wasn't until I heard a sermon that my former pastor, John Jenkins, preached in which he said that men have very basic needs — to feel respected, admired, and appreciated. That changed my entire approach, but it took me years to get there and lots of wasted energy on relationships that went south.

Daddy issues can cause us to develop unhealthy attachments. Sometimes we fall too hard too fast. Particularly if sex is involved, our emotions take control and our ability to make healthy decisions is lost.

Caroline, as discussed previously, was once a very good girlfriend of mine. She consistently fell too hard too fast. As soon as she made a connection she was in love whether it was reciprocated or not. They did not have to do much to earn her love, just a bit of attention was all she needed, very similar to the scenario that we discussed at the beginning of this book. But when things did not work in the relationship, she was severely crushed and once to the point of attempting suicide. The end of her relationships caused her to experience the same agony and despair she felt when her father passed away as a child. She never healed from her father's untimely death and each break up caused her to experience that death over and over again.

Daddy issues also cause us to get comfortable with the idea of being rejected, particularly from men. If our fathers did not spend consistent, good quality time with us, we may subconsciously feel a sense of rejection. Rejection issues are severe. We begin to not only attract but seek after those that will reject us. We look for the bad boys, the boys that live the fast life, or live out loud. We like the dope boys, the rappers, the flashy guys, professional athletes, the driver of the fanciest car, the guy with the fanciest clothes (swag), the frat guy, the club owners, the emotionally unavailable dudes, etc.

- 63% of youth suicides are from fatherless homes (US Dept. Of Health/Census) – 5 times the average.
- 90% of all homeless and runaway children are from fatherless homes – 32 times the average.
- 85% of all children who show behavior disorders come from fatherless homes – 20 times the average. (Center for Disease Control)
- 80% of rapists with anger problems come from fatherless homes –14 times the average. (Justice & Behavior, Vol 14, p. 403-26)
- 71% of all high school dropouts come from fatherless homes – 9 times the average. (National Principals Association Report) [2]

In potato salad, one of the key ingredients is mustard. It gives the dish a tangy and savory flavor. One can easily tell when potato salad does not have mustard because it has a white, bland color. Potato salad with mustard in it, however, has a yellowish tint. For many of us, that lets us know that we potentially have a flavor-filled batch of potato salad. As with mustard for potato salad, fathers bring the same quality to our lives and the statistics above prove that regardless of what we say, fathers in the home are important.

During my tenure as a wedding planner, I had a client that I adored. She was tall, beautiful, and very pleasant. She, Tiffany, was artsy and super sharp, quite possibly one of the most intellectual women I've encountered. Tiffany and her fiancé planned to marry within two months, so we had to move very quickly. During the planning, our professional relationship developed into a friendship that I valued. Our conversations regarding logistics would soon turn to conversations about life, social justice, and current events. She had such a keen sense of humor and her personality was a good balance of ratchet and professional class, which I adored about her. I noticed, during our conversations, that there were some factual inconsistencies. But, I know that I often get confused, so I paid it no mind. I loved to hear stories of her father's early activism and his role in the civil rights movement. I could tell by our conversations that she loved and admired her father. I saw the look in her eyes when she referred to him as "Daddy".

Tiffany's father and mother divorced when she was six years old. Shortly after the divorce, her dad moved to another city and then married a woman that Tiffany developed a complex relationship with. She admitted that, as a child, there were times that she felt her stepmother didn't seem to care much for her presence.

A short, plain guy with a scruffy beard, Tiffany's finance was a man of very few words. He rarely had anything to say or any ideas to share about the wedding. During the planning, I discovered that he would be her second husband. Her first marriage ended in divorce because of her ex-husband's extramarital affairs. After the divorce, Tiffany relocated and began dating her now fiancé.

As time progressed, things began to change. The closer we got to the wedding day, the more volatile the relationship between Tiffany and her fiancé became. There were times when he would not show up for planned meetings and when he would show up, the meeting would end up with a fight between the two of them.

On the eve of the rehearsal dinner, the day before the wedding, after the meal, I wanted to tie up a few loose ends with Tiffany, but I couldn't find her. I looked all over for this girl. I looked outside, in the kitchen, pantry, and everywhere else trying to find her. Finally, I found her in the parking lot with a face full of tears. At that moment, she confided in me that she had discovered that her fiancé had been cheating.

Wow!! I could only imagine how heartbroken she had to be to discover this only hours away from her wedding. I comforted her and prayed with her. I quietly wondered if she was still going to proceed. During the process, I kept my words brief about the relationship and never tried to comment on it. Looking back, I would have grabbed her and walked her to my car and driven off cancelling everything. But, I felt that it was her initiative to take and not my place.

The couple chose to get married that day and I was paid for my services. But sadly, the marriage did not last for long. It was filled with more lies, betrayal, disrespect, and a bunch of heartache. Eventually, the marriage ended in divorce after a year or so. You see, the problem was that she kept choosing men that treated her the same way that she perceived her father's love. She constantly kept repeating the cycle of rejection and abandonment that she experienced when her father left the family when she was six years old. For her, that's what she thought love from a man resembled. When we tell our children that their absent fathers love them, we damage them. We are actually saying to them that love doesn't put you first, love doesn't visit you, love doesn't honor their responsibility to you by paying child support on time, love doesn't protect your feelings, and love doesn't develop a relationship with you. And that is how the cycle of rejection gets repeated and passed down from generation to generation.

I adored Tiffany and we continued to communicate for quite a while. We would attend festivals together and have coffee from time to time. Then, I noticed that she had become quick to react and easy to take offense. Other people that had come to be in our circle began to notice it as well often asking, "what's going on with Tiffany?" I always shrugged my shoulders and would quickly change the conversation to prevent gossip. Then, one day, she grew cold and distant. I stopped hearing from her and she stopped taking my calls. I tried to reach out to her on several occasions to reconcile.

Every time I reached out, she continued to say things were fine and that we eventually would talk about it. We never had that conversation. I learned later from a mutual friend that she didn't feel that I supported her. I never gained a full understanding of what that meant.

For Tiffany, her relationships with her ex-husbands were traumatic for her and changed how she perceived the world and reacted to it. She became triggered when she perceived anyone or anything to be a threat to her or that made her feel rejected. It was a challenge for her to receive love from a healthy place because that notion was foreign to her. My dear friend Tiffany taught me that we have to first choose to heal from our past before we pursue loving relationships. Then, we must choose not to allow negative situations to change us for the worst.

Trauma changes our brain. "A traumatized brain is "bottom-heavy," meaning that activations of lower, more primitive areas, including the fear center, are high, while higher areas of the brain (also known as cortical areas) are under activated. In other words, if you are traumatized, you may experience chronic stress, vigilance, fear, and irritation. You may also have a hard time feeling safe, calming down, or sleeping. These symptoms are all the result of a hyperactive amygdala."[3]

Heightened fear, hypersensitivity, and thinking the worst of a situation is very common in dealing with emotional trauma. It can cause you to be super triggered. Particularly, if you are suffering from what I refer to as rejection syndrome, you see situations through the lens of your rejection. You have become sensitive to it. You are the first to notice when you are rejected and often quick to assume that you are being rejected.

For example, let's say you and several old college friends, while attending an event, discussed planning a trip together.

Later, you discover that you were not included in the text messages to plan the trip. Now some people may just chalk it up to believing they were left out by mistake. We all know that, as adults, we have a thousand things on our plate and can see how it may have slipped the person's mind to include you on the text or how they could have easily forgotten that you were a part of the initial conversation that took place at the event. However, if you suffer from rejection syndrome, you may, without hesitation, assume that the person that started the group text left you out because they secretly don't like you or they just don't want you to participate in the trip. We may never know what the truth is because we can never read what's in a person's heart. However, to think of it negatively is to bring torture and suffering to our soul. Why? Because the feeling that someone has rejected us is painful. Why suffer?

In addition, we may act out on our emotions if we feel rejected. If a person feels they were left out of a group trip, if they do decide to attend, they may distance themselves from the person they believe rejected them or behave defensively around that person. And other people will notice. Why spoil a perfectly great getaway? It is always better to think the best of a person's intentions until we know without a doubt otherwise. Choose to do what brings the most peace and causes us the least amount of harm.

In addition, people that have suffered from rejection syndrome tend to use rejection as a weapon. Because they know first-hand the pain, suffering, and the questioning of self that comes from feeling rejected, a person suffering from rejection syndrome will inflict the same type of pain on people that they feel causes them harm or stands in their way. They will purposefully not invite people to important events or try to leave them out because after all, hurting people hurt people.

There are so many other side effects that result from daddy issues such as being an overachiever to demonstrate our value, as my friend Kennedy explained in her quote at the beginning of the chapter. But, let me also be the first to tell you that there is beauty in being rejected! Most great people on this planet have suffered from rejection; Oprah Winfrey, Jesus Christ himself, Jay Z, JK Rowling, Jim Carrey, and the list goes on and on. I've known people that suffered rejection from their parents that grew up to be amazing parents. I have also met people that started successful businesses because they were fired by their employer. The best thing you can do for yourself is to learn to embrace rejection and to see its beauty. Rejection can be the thing that propels you to greatness!

Rejection can also serve as redirection to something better. I have met many people that were rejected by a lover and then went on to find their true love. I have literally looked back on my life and thanked God for the boyfriend that cheated on me. I believe that was God's way of saying, "I've got something better for you, sis." And as Joseph in the Bible stated after he was rejected and betrayed by his brothers that found him years later serving as the Governor of Egypt, "what you meant for evil, God meant for good." [4] From now on, instead of crying, let's look rejection in the eyes, embrace it, and find the purpose in it. It could quite possibly be the best thing that happens to you. Rejection can be your superpower!

Questions to Journal

Describe your relationship with your father?
How does your relationship with your father impact your relationship with men?
How does your relationship with your father impact you overall?

Describe a time that you felt rejected? How did you react?

Describe a time that you rejected someone whether it was a lover or friend? How did you want the rejection to make them feel?

Bullying

"Throughout my entire life, I have been short and skinny. During my teen years, while everyone was blossoming into a woman, I was stuck with a little boy build. Kids, especially hormonal teenage boys, spent a lot of time picking on my underdeveloped body. I spent a lot of time crying and self-loathing. As an adult, I am confident in my appearance but struggle with self-love at times. I can't help but think if I learned to love myself better and heard more words of affirmation at home, the blows of teenage bullies wouldn't have left scars that are visible today." Tahari S.

As with any culture, there is always the neighborhood bully. For the black community, bullying was a part of the culture growing up. Everyone had a "Deebo" in their community. Whether Deebo stole your bike, like the character in the movie *Friday*[1] or picked on you and called you names or heckled you on your worst possible day, the sting hurts. I've met many women of all ages that can still remember their Deebo, and bullying situations. It can be so devastating that the memory does not fade, and we carry it with us throughout our lives.

Being a victim of bullying can change us in numerous ways; For one, it makes us more aggressive. Typically, after being bullied we make the mental decision that we will never allow anyone to hurt us like that again. We replay the experience over and over in our head thinking of all the things we should have said or should have done. We think of other possible scenarios that could have happened to give us the upper hand. Then, we make the agreement with ourselves that if we are ever put in that situation again, we will win. So, the very next situation in which we feel resembles anything like our bullying incident, we are immediately triggered, our defenses kick in, and we act on the agreement we made with ourselves that we must win.

Recently, I witnessed two women arguing. During the argument, one woman proceeded to raise her voice. Suddenly, one of the women stood up and began to grit her teeth as she clenched her fists. Her face became red with anger. It was obvious to all in the room that she was furious. The argument escalated to the point that people had to step in between the two to separate them. It was crazy! Later, she shared with us that the argument took her back to a previous instance in her childhood or early adult life where she felt threatened or bullied. She promised herself that she would never let another bully win. So, for her, the way to win was to react. Instead of remaining calm during the altercation, her defenses were triggered and soon, she was on ready!

When we face a situation that causes us to return to our childhood behavior or brings up a painful childhood memory, that's when we have to realize that we are triggered. For many of us, we grew up believing that we must win the argument or throw the most shade to be the victor. We were trained that we must belittle our aggressors and make them feel hurt or ashamed to win. Please hear me — This is toxic behavior, my sisters. Hurting someone, in essence, to feel better about our position in life or to win a dispute is a clear indicator of an unhealed wound. I often tell my daughter that not every situation deserves our attention or our tears. And I think that is the same for adults that find themselves in heated situations- not everything deserves our energy and attention. As adults, we have to exercise some self-control and mature our emotions to a point that we can remain calm in the face of adversity. Quite frankly, we should be able to calmly sit in a room with someone we disagree with and hash it out politely without trying to damage their self-esteem.

Bullying hurts us to the core because it makes us feel small and inferior. Because of this, many adults that have been victims of bullying tend to rely on control. It's a way to assure they never feel overpowered again. A person that has been a victim of sexual abuse may internalize their abuse in a similar manner. A person that has been sexually abused or molested as a child may rely on sexual control as an adult. It is because they felt powerless in the situation and want to prohibit that feeling again.

Bullying and this need to be in control is maddening. The need to be in control causes us to become territorial. When we feel someone intrudes on our territory, we do what we can to push them out of the way. We become aggressive or super defensive. We also behave this way when we feel our voice is not being heard. Then the gossip starts so that we can get others on our team and against our opponent. The women on reality TV often reinforce this behavior. We have to develop positive coping skills.

The truth is, though, that when we feel threatened or unheard we do not need to become defensive and clap back. We have to realize that the ability to remain silent is more powerful than the ability to clap back. I used to praise the woman that would clap back the loudest or win the argument. Now, as I have healed and see things through a different lens, I praise the woman that has the ability to remain calm and walk away. Walking away requires self-control and confidence. The woman that can hold her head high, walk away, and choose not to engage in foolery is the winner in my book because she is choosing her peace over winning a silly argument. She realizes that she has nothing to prove to anyone and that her joy is not found in hurting or belittling someone.

Even as adults, we still have to deal with bullies. I have dealt with more than my share of bullies and I have acted as the bully. I realized that I bully when I feel threatened or rejected (definitely a trigger there). We also have to realize that the saying is true "hurting people hurt people". I finally came to the decision that I was going to heal myself so that I would not bully and that I was not going to allow bullies to ruin my day or to make me bitter.

I became a leader at a very young age. Not only was the power intoxicating to me, but I also abused it. I did not want anyone to hurt or challenge me, so I remained extremely guarded and as unapproachable as possible. I lacked any level of humility or compassion and saw myself as someone that simply doled out responsibilities and orders. I made every conversation about me and was always in a mode of self-preservation. And if you made me feel challenged in any way, I was sure to retaliate. Boy, I was savage!

That situation resulted in disaster when almost everyone in my department resigned, leaving me to do the work alone. From that situation, I learned that I needed to treat people the way I expected to be treated. If you are leading people, please understand that people do not want to be managed. No one grows up, completes college then says, "I can't wait to have a boss!" The best we can do is to exercise understanding and be a whole person before we take on that title. People should not have to work around our idiosyncrasies, immaturity, emotional baggage, and egos to have some peace at work. If we are quick to take things personally, led by our egos, ready to retaliate, and unapproachable we need to reconsider if this is our time to lead.

As a kid, I loved the biblical story of David and Goliath. In this story, a short and scrawny boy slays a giant that had been bullying a village for years. Prior to David, many people tried to kill Goliath with mass attacks and sophisticated weapons but to no avail. Then, along comes David who changed the game by using something no one else had used to defeat Goliath. It was something very simple- a sling and a pebble.

With that sling, he became the winner and defeated a giant that was far bigger than him. [2]

The same goes for our bullies. We are using the wrong weapons to conquer them. Typically, we fight back with verbal assaults, gossip, or slander. But we need to use a different, simpler tactic- love and understanding. I have never met a person on this planet that did not want to be loved.

We were made to love and to be loved. Often our bullies are crying out for love and acceptance. They want to be included, seen, or heard. They may have felt that they did not measure up to you, that you did not care for them, maybe they even felt disrespected by you. When I'm faced with bullies, my tactic used to be completely ignoring them- silent violence as I call it. I could behave as if an individual was completely dead to me. If I saw them, I would not say hello. If they walked by, I would quickly turn my head, so I would not see them. If I was in a room with them I would talk with everyone except them. Then I realized that ignoring them often makes it worse, trust me. No one likes to feel unseen. But reasoning with them can change the game. That person you despise that causes you pain that has bullied you can become one of your greatest allies if you choose love.

Now I can word spar with the biggest of bullies. However, I've found that it only allowed them to live inside of my emotions. Every time I heard their name, I would roll my eyes, cringe, or begin to gossip about them. It also gave the people on the outside power over me because they now knew who my kryptonite was. They knew they could get a rise out of me by mentioning that person or the situation. Whenever someone said, "let me tell what your girl did" I knew who they were talking about and the conversation was going to get me upset. When we were all in a room together, people who knew there was tension between us would watch to see how we would behave. It felt like the negativity kept living on and on. So, I began to try a different tactic- love. When I saw them, I would wave at them and say hello as if we had been friends for years. I would always greet them with a warm smile. I began to send kind text messages to them just to say hello and to see if they needed anything. It would totally catch them off guard because they would not expect me to behave like that. This was not the typical way that situations like this are handled. Eventually, it would calm and defuse the situation. Now you may look at this as the behavior of the weak. But I believe that this is choosing peace and healing for myself. There is not a person on this planet that is worth my peace or emotional health. Not one!

Questions to Journal

Were you bullied as a child? How did it impact you?

Describe an experience in which you were the bully as a child and as an adult? What caused you to react that way?

Describe an experience in which you behaved aggressively? What caused you to behave that way?

How can you respond to bullies in a healthy way?

How can you assure that you do not bully anyone else?

Failed Relationships

There is nothing like a romantic relationship that goes south to cause us trauma. Can you remember how you felt after your first major heartbreak? I can remember it so vividly. Oh gosh, I was devastated! It felt as if someone had taken a knife and stabbed it right through my heart. I can remember having an anxious stomach feeling and crying uncontrollably. I didn't think I would ever get over it.

What's worse is when we were the victim of some form of disrespect or betrayal within the failed relationship. There is nothing more gut-wrenching than to realize that a person we loved dearly did not love us the same way. And if they have chosen another woman, what a blow to our ego! Eventually, we move on but if we do not heal properly, that hurt remains inside and we will suffer. The trauma will plague us and impact how we relate to other male suitors. We will bring the baggage of the previous relationship into future ones.

A failed relationship can cause us to become insecure, jaded, desperate, and filled with loads of self-doubt. If I can be frank, we often blame ourselves for failed relationships, though we are not willing to admit it. Raise your hand if you have blamed yourself for a failed relationship. My hand is up. Though we spend quite a bit of time rehashing and analyzing the breakup with girlfriends over bottles of wine, internally we secretly blame ourselves; "Maybe if I was prettier", "if I was more easy-going", "if I was skinnier or if my booty was bigger", "if I knew how to cook better meals", or " if I gave better head, he would have stayed". This internal processing is so damaging to our self-esteem. Not only can it cause our self-esteem to shrink, but it can also make us bitter. We become angry with our ex-lover and ourselves. If not dealt with properly, the anger expands to all men and soon we can also become angry with the dating system, similar to

Caroline. I have met several women that are just bitter about dating. They find it a challenge and they find the way that black men, in particular, behave and select women to be a drag.

Now don't get me wrong, our brothers have some issues. If we take a deep dive into our history, we will see that men, not just brothers, often view women as mere conquests. I can recall, when I was a child, hearing my older male cousins talking about their sexual conquests, "you hit that yet?" "Yeah man, I told you I was gonna smash that." Then, they give high praise and celebrate the one that achieved the goal. Even today, this is still esteemed. I love hip-hop music, but many of the lyrics praise sexual conquests and who has the baddest chick. Ladies, we must realize that we have bought into this hook, line, and sinker because we support the music and follow suit with this type of logic. Many female artists proclaim and profess to be the baddest chick and another woman's worst nightmare. This adds additional trauma because it fuels the need inside of ourselves to compete with each other.

In addition to being attracted to rejection, my friend Tiffany was desperate for love. After her first divorce, she missed being in a marriage along with the security and stability that came with it. She wanted what I refer to as the "white picket fence life"- the marriage, the house, the two cars, the kids and the dog. She was not content with being a single mom and missed checking the box- married. Additionally, she never healed from her previous marriage. Her ex-husband's infidelities that occurred very early on in her development, damaged her self-esteem. Her damaged self-esteem and quiet desperation caused her to accept her fiancé then turned husband's blatant disrespect. She was, after all, accustomed to it. She married her husband regardless of all of the red flags that were right in front of her face. There is nothing wrong with the desire for love and companionship as long as we don't look for love out of our hurts.

Recently, I had abdominal liposuction (after carrying two kids I deserved it). I saw it as a simple out-patient procedure and didn't put a lot of thought into the recovery process. So, I continued to plan events and schedule my calendar accordingly. I did not realize until after the procedure that I needed to make time to heal. For the first week, I was exhausted and sore. Bending was a chore and walking swiftly was taxing. I was also super dehydrated. I realized that my body perceived liposuction as trauma and I needed to make the necessary time to heal. So, I canceled all of my plans to stay home and heal. I restructured my diet, took vitamins, and assured that I got plenty of rest.

After a failed relationship, it's good to take a break and do some healing. We need to resist the temptation to heal by jumping into a new relationship. I've been that girl that has gone from one failed relationship to the next. Trust me, it's not fun. It's like piling on layers of junk on top of junk. I brought this baggage into the new relationships unbeknownst to me. All of my insecurities that I had gained from the failed relationship followed me to the new relationship like a toddler following their mother, collecting more baggage. When I look back, I notice that my distrust for men, paranoia, and insecurities increased from failed relationship to failed relationship.

We need time to learn to forgive and repair the damage from the prior relationship. We need to do a check-up to see if we still have a healthy image of self. Seeking a therapist is always a good idea. Journaling can help as well. But, you must find the best method to heal that works for you. If not, you will bring all of the baggage and issues into a new relationship.

Before I began dating my husband, I took two years off from dating. I used that time to get to know myself, sort of like a detox period. During that time, I learned that I did not really like myself — the proof I had was some of the choices I made. I made irresponsible purchases that kept me in debt, I did things to people that I called friends that kept me in the middle of drama, and I dated men that were a true reflection of the rejection I experienced as a child. During that season in my life, I spent a lot of alone time with God and myself learning to love and to trust. I spent time in therapy and worked to build my self-esteem. When I met my husband, I can honestly say I was a whole person. I had a healthy self-image, a relationship with God, and love in my heart. The proof I had that I was on the road to healing — I truly loved my husband, but I still had enough love for myself that if the relationship could not serve us both, I had the ability to walk away.

Failed relationships also include friendships. After a friend betrays us or hurts us, it can cause us to feel inferior as well. It can also cause us to lose trust. There was a period in my life that I didn't trust friendships. I was angry when I felt they were not there for me and often questioned their loyalty. I was easily offended by the slightest thing they did that I deemed wrong. I offered no grace and understanding and was quick to cut people off. I realized that I had not healed from a previous friendship that had gone sour. My wounded emotions would not allow me to enjoy the friends that God placed in my life.

One thing we have to realize, as black girls, is that friendships require work to maintain. As we discussed previously regarding Shawna, we have to be upfront with our friends about our feelings and create an environment where they can be upfront with us as well. We must extend grace realizing that people are imperfect. We also have to set realistic expectations as well.

To maintain healthy friendships, we must change the way we view conflict. When we have a disagreement with our friend, we may view it as the end of the friendship and that is quite possibly because of our past experiences. The fact is that disagreements and conflict often solidify relationships. You each gain new insights about each other during conflicts. It also provides you with an understanding of your boundaries and that should help the friendship grow stronger. I must admit that I am often a bit leery of people when they claim that their friendships have never faced any trials or never had any conflicts. Where is the growth? We must not fear conflict as Shawna does but embrace it as we now know that conflict produces growth.

Questions to Journal

Describe a failed relationship that really hurt you. How did it make you feel? Did you take the time to heal from it?

How did the failed relationship change your view of relationships?

Death

In 2015, my older cousin passed away. Chelle was one of my favorite people on this planet. She was a 42-year-old mother of two young boys. A lively person with a very funny sense of humor, Chelle was warm and friendly and the kind of person that never met a stranger. She wasn't flashy or flamboyant and lived a very humble life never chasing riches or fame.

We were close, raised almost like sisters. When I was a kid, I was impressed by my cousin Chelle who was a teenager at the time. She would take me to the skating rink which allowed me to get to know all of her friends and boyfriend. I would listen to her talk with her friends about school, boys, music, and the latest fashion. She was my baby-sitter when I needed care, my go-to when I needed to laugh about something funny that happened at a family function, my confidant when I needed advice, and my protector when my parents tried to discipline me.

When I gave birth to my first child, my cousin became more like a supportive mother to me; encouraging me as I stumbled my way through motherhood without a clue. I called on her often seeking advice on nursing, illnesses, and other new mommy issues. Through it all, my beautiful cousin never judged me. She always encouraged me and told me what a good job I was doing.

On a warm day in September of 2015, death knocked on my cousin's door, made its way inside her home and further into her bedroom having a seat on her bed. Her last words to me were in a text before she began sleeping uncontrollably. I told her that we were all worried about her and she said she was worried as well. She texted, "I love you always and forever." Just like that, she was gone.

After her death, I struggled with understanding it for many years. There were days that I didn't believe that it happened — I now know firsthand that denial is a very powerful emotion. I would pick up the phone to call her with something funny to share, but later realizing she wasn't going to answer. Then, there were days when I became angry about the situation, while other days I just felt a big sense of hurt in my heart.

The most challenging part of all of this was that I found it so hard to believe that God would take away my cousin at such a young age while she had two small boys that needed her. It was much easier for me to accept death when my grandparents died. They were elderly, sick, and had lived long and eventful lives. But this was as if God had somehow made a mistake. In addition, my cousin wasn't a bad person and never caused trouble, so I just could not wrap my head around this. The thing about death is that it does not discriminate. Age nor race nor height nor weight or intellect are factors in determining who dies.

Because of her death, there was a time that I was completely changed. It made me think about my own mortality. Although it taught me not to take any moment for granted, it also increased my anxiety. I feared death like never before because I felt that it can happen to any of us at any time. It's not something that just happens to an elderly person. Having children or people in your life that need you will not stop death from knocking on your door. At one point in my life, I was extremely crippled by this experience; my kid got a cold, I panicked. My sister didn't answer her cell phone, I worried that she had been attacked. Because for me, death was always looming. If it could happen to my cousin, a good and decent human being, there was nothing to stop it from happening to any of us.

I questioned for the longest, why God? Why take her, my beloved cousin? I had to come to terms with the fact that there are just some things we will never receive the answer to in this life. Over time, I have learned to accept it. It happened, and I had to learn to be okay with it. I'll never have all of the answers. There will always be hurt in my heart. But I can't remain stuck. I began to look back at all of the blessings my cousin gave me and the fun times we had together instead of the sadness of her death. I'm glad I had her in my life for the time that she was here. Although I still miss her, I realize that she is in a better place than here on earth.

I also think that perhaps God may have been saving her from something. Perhaps she would have spent the rest of her life in physical pain and agony from her illness if she was still here. But again, I will never know the answer.

It is my belief that part of the pain that we experience during the death of a loved one is guilt. Death teaches us that we need to love and appreciate people while they are here. We should spend as much time with loved ones as we possibly can, play with our kids as much as we can, and say all of the things we need to say to family and friends before it's too late. We need to not waste precious time with petty disagreements that serve us no purpose. That takes away from the time that we should be loving on the people we care about. Resolve conflict swiftly so that we experience no guilt in the death of a loved one.

If you have experienced the death of a loved one, you know that it feels like there is a hole in your heart. That pain is tough to live with. Day in and day out, struggling to find peace or something to remove the pain.

I also find that coping with the loss of a loved one interrupts a good night's sleep. Those quiet moments at night when we are left alone with our private thoughts and nothing to distract us is when the pain in our heart intensifies. We hope that time will heal the pain and it certainly helps but until we deal with it, it never really goes away. It simply hides for a bit. What's even sadder is that we often adopt negative mechanisms to cope; addictions, overeating, co-dependency, anger, etc. We look at these devices because they are easy for us — easy to obtain and easy to use. They are at our disposal and they provide a short term means of comfort.

Sometimes, losing a loved one makes it hard for us to trust or love again. We fear that people will leave us the same way our loved one left us during their death. On the flip side, it can make us co-dependent. We love so hard out of fear, becoming all too clingy and too invested in the relationship too quickly because that person is now filling a void that they were not designed to fill. It's that smothering type of love that has the possibility of making a partner resentful.

Death is also scary for us because we do not know what is next. Our world is filled with so many assumptions about the afterlife and that can be overwhelming. Many of us view death as the end as if the person fell down some deep, black hole and we will never see them again. However, for believers of Christ, death is not the end. We know that death is just the beginning as it brings us to an eternity filled with great wonders, rest, and peace. Our focus should not be on the small amount of time we will spend on this earth but spending our eternity in heaven. That is our hope and the cornerstone of our faith.

I may never have all of the answers about my cousin's death. I will always wonder why God took her from us so early. There will always be a small hole in my heart for her. But I am at peace and know that she is in a better place and waiting for me on the other side. I am grateful for the time we spent together and the children she left behind that reminds me so much of her.

Questions to Journal

How has the death of a loved one impacted your life?

How did you heal from it?

What are your beliefs about the afterlife? How do your beliefs about the afterlife manifest in your daily life?

The Devil

Who is the devil? A creature in a red suit, with a pitchfork and a long tail —truly, that is not who the devil is. A magnetic, charming man dressed in a fine suit that comes to sweep a beautiful lady off her feet — could that be the devil? The ambition you have inside of you for riches and fame that caused you to work long hours of the day and night, miss your kids' soccer games, and neglect spending quality time with your spouse — could that be the devil? The small whisper in your ear that tells you to post something on social media that you know will hurt your friends' feelings — could that be the devil?

The devil comes to us in many forms. He is a spirit being, so he has the ability to camouflage himself and mainly it's in the form of our deepest desires or unhealed wounds that he personifies himself.

Every single day there is a war raging and that battle is for control of our very souls. Every choice we make determines who we will serve and who will reign and rule in our lives. The more bad choices we make, the more we welcome the devil and his influences to control our lives. The Bible states, "give no vent to Satan." When you make one bad decision, it opens the vent for Satan (the devil) to enter in. When he enters our lives, he causes us to make more bad decisions. That's his goal. The Bible also states, "the devil comes to kill, steal, and destroy."(John 10:10-29)[1] The devil comes to kill our joy, steal our peace, and destroy our purpose. He wants us to roam aimlessly throughout the earth with no sense of self, living unfilled lives doomed for disaster. And that starts with the simple decisions we make every day.

The devil's tricks are easy to identify. He tells us that the things that we read in the Bible are not real and cannot be trusted so that we won't follow God's plan. He tells us not to be kind and to focus only on our own self-preservation to make us difficult and bitter. He tells us to do things that hurt ourselves and cause harm to other people because he wants us and them to suffer. Every single day, he tries to use us to accomplish his goal of making people miserable. He causes us to hold grudges over things that really don't matter. We have to use wisdom to identify when the devil is trying to manipulate us and take us off course. Reading the Bible helps us to understand that because he will tell us to do the opposite of what God requires of us.

Not only do we have to read the Bible, we also have to understand the Bible and have a relationship with God for ourselves. The devil can easily use the Bible by misinterpreting scriptures as well to control us. Take a look at our history and you will see a lot of that. That's all the more reason that we must educate ourselves.

Questions to Journal

What decisions have you made that you regret?

What are some of the bad choices you have made in your life? What has caused you to make those? What has been the result of making bad choices?

How can we keep the devil out of our lives?

Chapter 2
The Healing Process

We have spent quite a bit of time examining our hurts and putting them on the table. Now it's time to heal. Before we move any further, you have to decide if you want to heal because healing changes you. It makes you less angry, less aggressive, and gives you peace. You will walk away from things that will cause you pain and may even identify your purpose because you will know who you really are. The choices you make from here on will be different because you are not making them out of hurts. It's a very peaceful way of maneuvering throughout the world and some people are not up for that. Some folks prefer drama and negativity. Drama can become an addiction, particularly if that's been the sum total of your human experience. But you have to decide and now is the time.

Self-Awareness

You cannot fix what you are unaware of. The healing process begins with self-awareness, which is basically understanding who you are, your hurts, your triggers, strengths, and weaknesses.

In my opinion, self-awareness is a lifestyle. It's constantly checking your emotions and triggers to see what areas are unhealed. We need to search our hearts and examine our ideals and motives to know where we need to begin our healing work.

Once I worked at a government consulting firm where I was hired as a marketing rep. We had several projects that required us to do direct mail campaigns. During one particular campaign that was led by a colleague of mine, I mentioned how I despised doing direct mail and that it not only bored me but annoyed me. My colleague was upset with me about the comment. I didn't understand why she was upset. We had all complained about how we did not like the direct mail aspect of the job from time to time including her. But she took it personally because this project was hers and she felt that I was criticizing her project. The truth was, I was attacking the overall process and how direct mail should not be part of the marketing process at all. It had absolutely nothing to do with her and everything to do with the work we had been assigned to do by our superiors.

I believe one of the most powerful tools in our healing toolkit is self-awareness. This is where the soul work begins. We need to check ourselves when we are faced with a situation that hits our emotions and triggers us. That is typically an indicator that the situation has awakened one of our unhealed emotional wounds. We need to ask ourselves which wound this situation has aroused. In the example above, perhaps my colleague hated being criticized and it caused her to react.

She chose to make that comment about her and I may never understand the reasoning behind it.

Let me share with you another example: I become very defensive when I feel that my freedom to make my own decisions is taken from me. I do not like to be pushed into doing things or making a decision. It reminds me of the overbearingness I faced during my childhood years. So, when I feel that way, I become terribly defensive, aggressive, and will even sabotage the situation. I will do anything I can to get the overbearing person away from me. I'm telling you it's a situation, y'all.

Taking things personally is a choice and it means you made that comment or situation about you. Just as my colleague made my comment about her and her specific project or when I make someone's behavior that I deem "pushy" about me. When we take things personally, we are actually internalizing the situation and adding more pain to the wound.

Here are some questions we need to ask ourselves before we take things personally:

Am I assuming the situation is about me?

Is this a human being human (a flawed individual like myself that is prone to make mistakes)?

Am I holding them to an expectation they are unaware of?

Did I do something to cause them to react this way?

Does this person truly mean to harm me?

Is this an unhealed wound inside of me that needs my attention?

When we take something personally, typically we take the next step to be offended by it. When we are offended, it means we have put thought into the situation and made a decision to be upset, hurt, or angry. My husband always says, "being offended is a choice." Sometimes it can be a harmless comment that was made but we become upset or angry by it. Sometimes it's just not about us- perhaps the person is having a bad day and we ended up the target, maybe they have some unhealed wounds that need to be addressed as well. I have seen so many friendships die because of taking something minor personally.

I was once a member of my local chapter of a social organization for black women. On one occasion, I told the president of that chapter that I was taking a hiatus from the organization. She politely said "okay," and wished me the best. I was furious at her response. "How dare she behave so cool when I tell her that I'm leaving after I have given so much of my time and effort to this organization," I thought. So, before I left, I texted her to explain that I was unhappy because she was so cavalier about me taking the hiatus. I told her that at a minimum she should show some concern and ask why I needed the hiatus. Of course, the president was completely caught off guard and didn't understand why I was so hurt but she sought to be as understanding as she possibly could. What she did not know was there was some history behind my feelings. I had become offended by a simple, harmless comment she made to me at a meeting several months prior. Instead of addressing my hurt directly with her at that time, I made it about me, took it personally, over-analyzed it, bottled it up, and replayed it in my head over and over for days. I was quick to believe she meant harm and the goal of her comment was to attack me. From that comment, I measured her like for me and assumed she secretly hated me. All along, she had no clue how I felt and I had no clue how she really felt.

What I chose to do next with my feelings really showed my level of emotional immaturity at that time — I picked up the phone and discussed my hurt feelings with some of the other members of the chapter and I knew exactly who to go to. I went straight to the other ladies that secretly hated her out of their own personal pain — negative people attract negative people. We had a great time bonding and connecting as we belittled this woman behind her back. The thing about this level of negativity and toxic behavior is that it knows no end and it just keeps growing and growing. The more we talked, the angrier we got, and our circle grew.

Then we started to attach negative meanings to every little thing this woman did. Discreetly, we ganged up on her and did our part to sabotage her and every single thing she did for that organization. Every step she took to make our chapter better and every decision she made, we found something wrong with it but did very little to help. When we got together, we discussed her and picked her apart, we even went as far as discussing her career, children, and husband who were completely innocent. We were mothers, in our thirties behaving like school girls. When I saw her, I tried to be as impolite and brief with her as I possibly could hoping that she would do something that I could add negativity to so that I could have more fuel for my toxic discussions about her. Because, to me, it was much more fun to be angry with her than to be kind. When I posted something about her in the group text, everyone responded quickly, and I enjoyed that. As I look back on that situation in my hindsight, I realize what a vicious fool I was. I allowed something so minor to make me behave with such venom.

When I look back, I realize this woman had actually been kind to me. She gave me a gift for my daughter and offered me advice. If I said I was sick, she would check on me. She was forgiving when I dropped the ball on the responsibilities I had volunteered for. She was kind to me and I returned it with venom. It makes me sick to my stomach to think about my actions and how easily influenced I was.

The reality of it is, my unhealed wounds, generational trauma, and personal history interpreted her actions as negative. I was a victim of my own overthinking and it made me a very toxic person in that instance. I didn't have the conflict management skills and maturity to resolve it. So, I relied on what I knew which was my learned behavior of tearing a person down. She lived in my emotions. Everything she did, I reacted to it. I could clearly articulate why this woman should be despised. I justified why we all should be mad at her and why she was not only a bad president but an overall bad person. The behavior that I displayed is a prime example of a person that completely lacks self-awareness, had taken things personally, and lacked conflict management skills.

Another part of self-awareness is realizing that we may have expectations of other people that are harmful to ourselves and our relationships. I used to exhaust myself because I had expectations of other people. I would be offended if someone did not show up for my parties or if they did not have the time to listen to me vent about my work issues. I expected that if I did something for someone, that they would have my back to the same degree. It was as if I felt that if I did a good deed, I had a pass to get something back from them. I was keeping score and distributing IOUs. But the harmful part was that they had no clue. Often, we have expectations of others that we have not communicated to them. Sometimes we do something for someone then expect them to be there for us, at all times — to come running when we need them, to comfort us, or to be the listening ear wherever and whenever we need it.

I had to learn the very hard way to expect nothing from anyone. Then, I would not be hurt. When I let go of the expectations, I was no longer disappointed, and my relationships survived. I realized that people are human beings and are going to make mistakes. I had to realize that I was the one that was being unfair to them with my unwritten expectations.

Another harsh truth that I had to embrace- human beings are selfish, including myself. And I had to accept that it's okay. I am a very compassionate person and I love hard so it hurts me when someone that I care deeply for doesn't show up for me. While I still believe that showing up is very important, people aren't always going to put me first and come running the second that I call.

Previously in my career, I worked with an older woman. We were both directors within a rather small organization. Our offices were positioned right next door to each other. We would sometimes chat and exchange small talk throughout the day. We were pleasant and friendly enough. Behind my back, however, she would initiate lengthy, negative conversations about me and my department. When I was not present, she encouraged my best staff members to leave my department to join hers. She would send emails discussing my projects, my work, and my department as a whole in a very negative manner to our superiors. I can clearly recall one of her emails she said, "her work is below the standard for this organization." She was a piece of work!

In the beginning, when she initially demonstrated this behavior to me, I took her attacks personally. I felt that she owed it to me to be kind and so I became offended. And I did what we always do when we are offended, I reacted. Fighting back in emails and engaging in a war of words with her became part of my daily routine. We then became known around that small office as enemies. It was toxic and exhausting. Every day, I would come home from work to my husband and kids and instead of focusing my attention on them I would spend time rehashing all of the things she had done that day and how I fought back. I would make them listen as I analyzed every detail of her behavior and actions.

Then, one day, miraculously, I made the decision that I was not going to be offended by her actions. I realized that her actions had nothing to do with me and that they were more about her, her unhealed wounds, and past experiences. I also came to the realization that my expectations of her needed to change — she did not owe me kindness or love. She wasn't a friend or a family member or even my sister in Christ. She was, in essence, a stranger in my life. So, therefore she did not owe me loyalty. Yes, those things would be great to have and make for positive relationships, but she did not need to give that to me.

When I embraced these truths, it empowered me to simply walk away when she would have her usual outbursts or fits around the office. From then on, when I would see a nasty email from her or hear about her antics that were directed towards me, I chose not to let it bother me. I knew it had nothing to do with me. Then, I began to notice a change in the perception of our relationship amongst my co-workers; Instead of them assuming us as enemies, she became known as the office troublemaker and I was removed from the equation all because I chose to no longer engage. I now had peace at work and at home.

Taking things personally is so harmful and toxic to our souls. When we take things personally, it causes us to feel rejected, inadequate, or ashamed. These feelings wreak havoc on our self-esteem. When we take things personally, we are making the choice to allow new unhealed wounds to develop. The next time you feel the desire to take something personally ask yourself the above questions. That will help you decide your next steps.

Questions to Journal

Think about some of the critical moments that have occurred in your life over the past six months that caused you to feel a negative emotion- anger, hurt, ashamed, humiliation, rejection, inferiority, etc. Why do you believe you felt that way? Can you recall experiencing that feeling in the past or in your childhood?

Jot down some expectations that you have of people you are in relationships with (i.e. friends, co-workers, superiors, family members, etc.). Are they aware of those expectations? Do you feel those expectations are realistic?

Action Items

For the next 30 days, pay attention to your emotions. Take note of the situations that cause you to feel offended. Purpose to not take offense.

Forgiveness

Forgiveness is a term that has become cliché. It's a term that every single wellness guru, preacher, pastor, spiritualist, priest, therapist, and life coach on the planet spouts. The funny thing is, although I have heard this term mentioned quite a bit, I had a hard time understanding what it meant. For so long, I struggled with what forgiveness looks like. All of my healing work kept hitting a brick wall because I lacked forgiveness. When you lack forgiveness, bitterness forms and you can become jaded about life. During the time that I harbored unforgiveness, I was quick to think the worst of a person's intentions and I loved to gossip. To be released from the bitterness, I had to forgive the one person that hurt me the most. For over fifteen years, I had been working to forgive them but could not release it because I did not understand what it was or the requirements on my part to make forgiveness work.

First, I had to understand what forgiveness is not — it's not a feeling. I can recall saying to myself, "I feel like I've forgiven them." However, I was quick to react when they said something that I deemed hurtful which was an indicator that unforgiveness was still present.

I also used to think that I had forgiven when I said, "I'm over it!" It's funny how we say this and think there is some magical power in those words.

Forgiveness is certainly not waiting for the offender to say I'm sorry. That apology may never occur.

Forgiveness, at its core, is a choice that we make daily over and over again. In every instance, it's deciding to let it go. Forgiveness includes choosing to immediately kick out the negative thoughts that pop up in our minds about that person or situation that has hurt us.

Many of us have been hurt in our past by someone that we felt let us down. That hurt can change our ideas about life and who we are. That's where the forgiveness journey begins.

I started my journey of forgiveness by writing down what the person did to me and mourned the situation one last time. I sat down one night and said to myself, "okay Nij, this is it. Let it out because this is the last time you are going to cry about this situation." I cried and mourned then wiped my face and told myself that from this day forward there will be no more tears and no more negative thoughts. This was easier said than done. There were moments when I found it difficult to control the negative thoughts about that person, but I persisted.

Next, I took the piece of paper that I had written down the offenses and visualized myself putting it in God's hand. I breathed in a big gulp of fresh air as I prepared my heart and mind for new beginnings, days without the chains of unforgiveness and bitterness weighing me down and jading my perspective. From that day forward, I chose forgiveness and by choosing forgiveness I chose myself because it freed my heart and soul from years of pain.

Now in my journey to forgive there are times when negative thoughts about the situation or person appear in my head. I've learned over time to immediately replace the thoughts with memories of the best parts of that person and to give them the benefit of the doubt. As an example, my absent father, I chose to forgive. There were many other circumstances that caused him to be absent. He suffered terribly in the Vietnam War and developed an addiction. He didn't have the tools to cope with life and particularly fatherhood. When I look back, it was in my best interest that he wasn't there. I was loved and supported by other men in my life that helped me to develop into a whole adult. Now don't get me wrong, I certainly had scars because of his absence. But I was able to rely on my inner strength and my relationship with God to heal. The scars also gave me a purpose in life- to help other women heal from rejection. I don't think about his absence or his rejection. When I do think of him, I choose to think about the conversations we had during his final days on this earth and how he told me he wished he could have walked me down the aisle on my wedding day. It's the positive stuff that I recall or nothing at all.

One thing we need to realize is that people are human. And being human means they are going to fail us. They are going to make mistakes gosh even huge mistakes. We can hold a person accountable for their actions while still extending forgiveness. When someone causes us harm, it's not the actual act that harms but also the lack of forgiveness that can be damaging as well. Forgiveness lasts far longer than the act.

How do I know when I have truly forgiven?

You will know that you are moving towards forgiveness when you realize that the situation or person that hurt you no longer controls your emotions. You are no longer triggered by that pain or any situation that resembles that pain. It no longer causes you to feel anger or hurt. The sting is gone. You are now numb to it. You no longer spend time mulling it over in your mind. Your view of the person that hurt you also changes. Instead of wishing them harm or waiting for them to suffer, you become indifferent towards anything that happens to the person that caused the offense. You have officially let it go.

Let me give you another example of forgiveness in action — many years ago, I had a former boss that I worked for. She was a mean, bitter, and brutal woman. She micromanaged, yelled, slammed doors, and bullied us into respecting her. What was worse was that she used email as her way to intimidate. She would send you an email letting you know when you were on her "list" and would cc herself to assure you knew she was documenting your behavior. Every meeting we had with her was stressful and filled with tension. This woman's cruelty used to bring tears to my eyes.

Years later, after she and I both went our separate ways, she found me on LinkedIn and wrote a note asking me to submit her resume to my current employer for one of our vacant roles. I responded politely to her, made small talk, and sent the resume as she suggested (it was not a management level position). Had I not been in a place of forgiveness, I would have refused to send her resume or ignored her email. I was indifferent to what happened to her and the feelings I previously had towards her no longer existed.

Here is something to consider- sometimes the person we need to extend forgiveness to is ourselves. We can be viciously angry with ourselves for mistakes we have made in the past; the abortion we had, the cheating on our mate that we participated in, dropping out of college, the affair we participated in, not showing up when a friend or family member needed us, or being a subpar parent. We can blame ourselves even for the unkindness of others- feeling as if we deserved it or did something to cause it.

Unforgiveness can also lead to us experiencing feelings of shame because of the decisions and choices we have made. Shame has the ability to cause us to feel deeply insecure. At any rate, forgiveness still needs to be extended to ourselves in the same manner that we extend it to others. If you feel you have not forgiven yourself, then you may need to stand in the mirror, look yourself in the eyes, and tell yourself you are forgiven. Write down what you need to be forgiven of, close your eyes, and picture yourself putting that piece of paper which now represents the situation in God's hands. Tell yourself over and over that you are loved, valued, and forgiven. There is no pain that cannot be healed and absolutely nothing we can't be forgiven of.

Now after reading this you may say ask yourself, "why should I forgive? Why should I let the person off the hook for what they did to me?" Honey, let me tell you that unforgiveness not only produces bitterness but causes anger too. Girl, do you realize that anger is addictive? It sure is. I have a family member that is addicted to anger. She gets angry about everything. If someone says something that she deems out of line, she quickly becomes angry about it. If someone cuts her off in traffic, she becomes angry about it. If her friend disagrees with someone, she becomes angry about it even though the situation has nothing to do with her. What's interesting about that is that often her friend will reconcile with the person she disagreed with and move on but my family member will continue to hold on to the grudge and the anger. If her ex-husband begins dating a new woman, she becomes angry with her because she is now dating her ex. Go figure. She never lets anyone off of the hook and remains in a perpetual state of anger. Anger is now a part of her daily life and is her go-to. She is known as the person in the family with an uncontrollable temper and the one who is ready to tell someone off or put someone in their place instantly. She hits far below the belt when she argues with someone. With her mouth, I have seen her humiliate and hurt people. It has robbed her of joy, emotional freedom, and healthy relationships. That is what unforgiveness will do to you. It makes you the person that you never intended to be.

Forgiveness, on the other hand, makes you free to love. You see the best in everything and have the ability to see the greatest potential in the people around you. And because your mind is not filled with negativity and you are focused on the positive things, you will begin to see the potential in yourself. Some have even said their anxiety has diminished after embracing forgiveness. It's worth it to embrace forgiveness.

Questions to Journal

Who has hurt you the most in your life?

How do you feel when you think of them or the hurt they caused you?

Who do you need to forgive right now?

Why is it hard for you to forgive them?

Action Items

For the person that hurt you or the person you need to forgive, mourn that situation one final time and write their name down along with the situation on a piece of paper. Picture yourself giving it to God. Journal how you feel.

Make a commitment to yourself that you will only think positive things every time you think of that person that caused your harm or nothing at all.

Contentment

Discontentment- lack of contentment; dissatisfaction.
A restless desire or craving for something one does not have.
A malcontent.[1]

"Why are they so popular?", "Why do they have this
house?", "How did they get to take that vacation?", "How did
they earn that degree?", "Why did they get to have a child
and I didn't?", "Why did they get married and I didn't?",
"Why did they get that job and I didn't?" All of these
questions are typically asked by a discontent person. A
discontent person focuses on what they don't have instead of
what they do have. They look at what other people have and
become frustrated because they do not have something equal
to or better.

Being discontent causes jealousy, envy, unhappiness, lack of
peace, anxiety and low self-esteem. Discontent people are the
true shade throwers and the fiercest one-uppers. They often
get angry and act out for no real reason. They want to see the
worst happen to people. A discontent person loves drama and
it's because they do not have joy or self-love.

Speaking of self-love. Many people talk about self-love. I've
often asked what self-love is because it's a term that has
almost become cliché. One thing I can tell you is that self-
love starts with contentment. We must learn to be content
with every single area of our lives. Now that does not mean
that we do not have things we want to change about
ourselves or upgrade within our lives. But it means that even
if those things do not change we are okay, we are happy with
our lot in life- content.

I can recall a time when I was single and desperately wanted to be married. You can just say I was pressed! It was all I thought about all day, every day. I wanted what I refer to as the white picket fence dream- the husband, the house, two cars, two kids, and the dog. At the time, many of my friends were getting married and I began to feel that God had forgotten about me. I couldn't be happy for my friends because I was so focused on me and my unfilled needs. I was discontent, and it made me sad. Then, suddenly, the sadness turned to anger. The desire to be married took over my emotions and I became irritable and snappy.

Soon, I realized that I had made marriage my idol and it was slowly spiraling me into a mild depression. I had to learn to not just be alone but be okay with being alone. So, I began to take myself out on dates, journal, and exercise. I pursued another degree and found a job that allowed me to travel. I joined social groups to meet new friends and read books to make me whole. I sought therapy and began to heal some of my traumas. I became involved with my local church volunteering to work with the widows and to serve some of the most elderly members of the church. I took my mind off of my needs and began to focus on serving the needs of others. Then, one day I looked up and there he was. The kindest man I have ever met. Thirteen years, two kids, and two mortgages later, we are still thriving.

I am fascinated by the Biblical account of the Apostle Paul. He was a high-ranking Roman citizen, a descendant of a wealthy and privileged background that was ferociously dedicated to persecuting the Christian church. One day out of the clear blue, he was struck blind for three days after hearing the audible voice of God. After Paul's encounter with God, he converted to Christianity and developed a love for God and the church. In summary, a man that hated Jesus so much that he tortured and killed many Christians in mass eventually became the person that loved Jesus so much that he wrote more than half of what we now refer to as the New

Testament.[2] That is simply amazing! Only God can change hearts.

In the book of Philippians, Paul states, "for I have learned in whatever situation I am, to be content."[2] After Paul began to follow Jesus with his whole heart, he left his wealthy possessions and status behind to spread the gospel of Christ. On this journey, he faced hunger, homelessness, and even jail. And here he is saying that through it all, he learned to be content in every situation regardless of what was going on in his life. He had peace that only God can give us. Understanding the life of Paul, made my frustrations with not being married seem so trivial compared to what Paul faced but yet he was content and here I was not dealing with half the stuff he dealt with, yet I was discontent.

The journey to becoming content starts with acceptance. Let's say you are in a bad marriage. You have to accept the fact that you are in it. You have to be okay with the fact that the situation happened to you. Then move forward to take steps to change it. It's also acknowledging the good that came out of that situation. Maybe the bad marriage produced beautiful children, maybe you got to travel because of it. Acceptance is choosing not to focus on all of the things that are wrong but what's right. From all of the drama that I experienced in my life (especially in my twenties, Whew Chile, I was wild one) I realized that it was all for a purpose. Because of the mistakes I made, I'm a better mother. I can use the wisdom I've gained from my mistakes to provide advice and guidance to others to keep them from committing the same mistakes.

There was a period in my life where I would wake up in the middle of the night and cry about my cousin's passing. I would lie awake night after night questioning God. My crying at night would impact my days because I would be too tired to function from being up so late. I also suffered from migraines from crying so much. During one of those sleepless nights, my spirit was so restless because the hurt I felt about my cousin's death was so heavy. Suddenly, I opened my eyes and out of nowhere I saw the words written in the darkness, but in plain sight, "*God grant me the serenity to accept the things I cannot change...*" When I saw those words, it was like an elbow punched me in my spirit to get my attention. At that very moment, I discovered a very simple answer to a complex problem that I was facing- --I can't change it, so I need to accept it. No matter how many nights I lie awake tormenting myself, it wasn't going to change it. My tears would not bring my cousin back to life. At that point, I accepted that she was gone. I let her go and soon began to sleep again at night.

What is your purpose? This is important because this another area that contentment is also derived from. Contentment is realizing that there is a reason we were put on this planet. It's seeking to identify and connect with that reason every day. Having a relationship with God and a positive heart helps us to realize our purpose.

One sure-fire way to tell if you are discontent is if you compare yourself to other people. Comparisons are the arch-enemy to contentment. And our beloved social media outlets only aid us in the comparisons. People tend to only post their best moments on social media- jet-setting, beautiful weddings, obtaining promotions, starting businesses, etc. I have been a victim of social media comparisons as well. I can recall when I was pregnant, I would hop on social media and see other expecting women that were glowing with minimal fat or cellulite. Yet, I wasn't so lucky. I gained weight and retained water in every part of my body that retention was possible. My skin tone changed while my nose spread like a river. That made me chalk my pregnancy up to horrible and made me sad. I could not focus on the fact that I was blessed to have the ability to carry life and deliver my child into this world because I was focused on what I thought I should have looked like based on what I saw on social media. My sisters, the thing about social media is that there is an element of control there and that control allows people to post the images based on the perception they want to give off. They only want to show you their fake social media life, not their real life. Folks rarely post their worst moments or bad days. There is an allusion that you can paint on social media- that every day is great in your life.

Recently, I had a friend who posted pics of her gorgeous wedding on social media. It was by far beautiful and she was indeed a gorgeous bride. We both have a mutual, single girlfriend that saw the pics and called me to say she wanted a wedding just like that. That wedding seemed like a fairytale to her that she could not obtain. She wanted the husband, the gown, the bridal attendants, the honeymoon, and everything else that she saw on our friend's page. "Why haven't I found Mr. Right? I want this!" Is what my friend said during our conversation. I realized that my friend was discontent. I'm sure she was happy for our friend, but she also wanted that for herself and could not focus on our friend's happiness because she was focused on her own. That, my friends, is where envy starts. We have to check those feelings immediately using our self-awareness so that we don't fall into the trap of envy. Later that year, the friend that had the beautiful wedding filed for divorce. You see, all we see are the beautiful images on social media, but we never truly know what is behind the images. It's important to remain focused on our own lives and be grateful for what we have.

Another sign of a discontented person is one who is chasing wealth, fame, or riches. Don't get me wrong, there is nothing wrong with wanting to be successful but when the desire consumes us and it becomes a primary focus, there lies a deeper issue. This type of person is empty and trying to fill a void. They are trying to prove to the world they are successful and worthy of acceptance. It's not the fame or money that they seek, but the validation that they hope to gain from it. They hunger for accolades and affirmation. It never fills the void and it will not make a person feel accepted. God did not design us to chase earthly wealth and riches. And it is destined to lead us to further discontentment because chasing material possessions only leads to wanting more material possessions. It's lust at its finest and you will never feel full. We must learn to accept ourselves and spend time building a relationship with our Creator, loving others, and finding our purpose.

Questions to Journal

What areas of your life are you dissatisfied with?

Why are you dissatisfied with those areas?

What are some of the positive things that have come from the dissatisfied areas of your life?

Have there been times in your life that wealth and/or fame was a major focus? Why?

Action Items

For the next two weeks, think about all of the positive things that have occurred in your life.

Chapter 3
Soul Cleanse

Your soul consists of your mind, will, and emotions. Your mind is the most powerful of the three because it powers the other two. The way that data is interpreted in your mind determines how you behave and react- fight or flight. The way that data is interpreted also determines how you feel about situations. In order to change our behaviors, we need to cleanse our souls.

The soul is really the core of who we truly are. The problem is that we spend so much time feeding our flesh (spending money on cars, clothes, food, and watching movies and TV) that we do not spend the same amount of time feeding our soul. Therefore, we do not know who we are. Have you ever found yourself buying something to impress people or to show you have arrived? That's a soul problem.

There is a painting at the Brooklyn Museum of Art called *Soul in Bondage*. This painting features a being with wings who is loosely shackled with a look of despair written across his face. In my opinion, this painting represents the torment that our souls are often involved in; the shame, the gluttony, the anxiety, the negative thoughts that plague our minds, the stress, the anger, the guilt, the feeling of powerlessness — all of these things keep us in bondage.

Do you want to know who you really are? Take inventory of the thoughts your mind produces throughout the day. Your mind is like a garden. Whatever type of seeds you choose to plant is what will take root and spring forth in your heart and will come out of your mouth and impact your decisions and actions. If you plant tomato seeds in your garden, you will get tomatoes not cucumbers. The same for your mind. If you fill it with negative thoughts your actions and attitude will produce negativity. I'm convinced that the happiest people on the planet love God, love themselves, think positive thoughts, and make the choice not to gossip.

Cleanse your soul by eliminating negative thoughts. Any counterproductive thought, not filled with love and not directing you to a purpose-filled life, get rid of it. Make a commitment that you will no longer entertain negative thoughts, even if they are true. Release it. No need to torture yourself. Even if someone harms you, recall the best of times with that person. Typically, you added them to your life for a reason. Focus on that.

On the very rare occasion that I do make potato salad, I call only two trusted people for a recipe — my mom (this girl makes the bomb potato salad, y'all) and my friend from the West Indies. I follow their recipes to a tee to make some of the best potato salad you have ever tried. Though it's still a pain to make, their recipes have never once failed me. So, it is as we are trying to change our behavior. We need a recipe that has proven to provide success and that is the Bible. This is the best recipe for our lives. I used to see the Bible as a strict tool that restricted my behavior with a bunch of rules that I was not even going to try to follow. Over time, I realized that the Bible is not a tool of strict rules but the opposite- it's actually liberating. The Bible is God's way of providing guidance to very flawed human beings. You still have free will to do what you want. But this is God's way of saying He wants the best for us and giving us direction just as a father guides and provides wisdom to his child. I realized if I had followed the Bible and waited to have sex with the person I would spend the rest of my life with I would have saved myself a bunch of heartache and soul ties. If I had learned to forgive instead of seeking revenge, I would have saved myself a lot of bad karma. If I had learned to love God and myself instead of looking for love from everyone else I would not have suffered so much emotional trauma.

What makes the Bible so unique is that it is filled with scriptures and words of wisdom that can help to change our lives and thought patterns. For example, when I read the verse that says, "all things work together for the good…," it completely changed the way I perceived the bad things that occurred in my life. It helped me to see that those bad things happened for a reason and not to focus on the bad thing that happened to me but to find the reason God allowed it to happen. When I changed my focus, I began to see the good in the absolute worst of situations. It helped me to see the situations and people that I once considered bad were actually beneficial to me. I'm now grateful for the old boyfriend that cheated on me because it made me appreciate my thoughtful, selfless husband. Because of the woman that disrespected me at work, I learned to deal with difficult people and to handle adversity with maturity.

Let me tell ya', there was a point in my life where I was the meanest and most difficult person in the room. But once I began to read the scriptures and internalize them, it completely changed my behavior. And my behavior changed because I used the Bible to cleanse my soul. I learned how to handle conflict by understanding that "a soft answer turns away wrath,"[1] and when I feel inferior I remember that "greater is He that is in me than He that is in the world."[1]

Whenever I am faced with a challenge not only do I pray, but I turn directly to the scriptures. It gives me a sense of peace and calm because I now know how to fight my battles. I no longer have to worry about getting in my own way because I have tools for success.

Have you ever driven in your car and felt the desire to ride without the radio turned on? Have you ever felt the need to sit in silence? That is your soul yearning for stillness and quiet time. I have learned over the years how essential it is to just sit in silence. It allows me time to gather and control my thoughts. It also allows me to hear from God. God is always speaking to us but it is difficult to hear from Him when we have so much noise in our heads. My silent moments typically consist of me releasing the worries of the previous day and thanking God for a new day filled with new opportunities. It allows me to take notice of the fact that I have a heart, lungs, and a brain that all function and allow me to be alive to enjoy each day.

Questions to Journal

What is your view of the Bible? What has shaped your view?

What do you to gain peace in your life?

Action Items

Find a Biblical scripture that resonates with you (see the Appendix). Meditate on it for a week.

Commit to kicking out negative thoughts for the next two weeks and only think positive thoughts.

Community

Positive friends are just as vital as positive thoughts. Over the years, I have drained myself with friends that love to gossip and as they say, "the dog that brings a bone, carries a bone." I learned that the hard way. I have also drained myself with friends that caused trouble, friends that really did not care if my family or I lived or died, friends that consistently made poor decisions, friends that took the smallest things personally, and friends that did not appreciate me as a person/friend. They competed against me and would throw slight shade. Bad friendships affected my thought life and how I behaved. They told me what I wanted to hear, gave me bad advice, held grudges, and were jealous of me and everyone else around. One of the things I have learned is that when people are jealous sometimes they will do things to quietly sabotage you and anything you are trying to achieve. You are sabotaging yourself by keeping negative friends around. Negative friends spread their toxicity like a plague.

Pay attention to how the friends that you keep impact your life. If you notice that you suddenly become involved in drama because of new people in your life, it means it's time to re-evaluate those friendships. If you start to notice that you gossip more or start to view life through a negative lens, again that is an indicator that it may be time to re-evaluate those relationships. Please note that friendships that are built on gossip do not last because eventually, that gossiping friend will soon begin to gossip about you. The slander they are spewing with you is telling of who they are.

I have also drained myself by entertaining opportunist friends. These friends were selfish and thirsty for ambition. These are the friends that only post pictures of you on social media if it tells the world something positive about them. Everything is about their benefit and every conversation is about them proving themselves to be great to the world. As a friend, you will find yourself sacrificing your time and emotional health often to make their dreams come true, yet they have little concern for what is going on in your world. They have not found contentment yet and will be quick to belittle yours. Their condescending remarks and selfishness will drain you and leave you emotionally broke.

There was also a time that I filled my life with relationships that I like to call "empty friendships". They weren't negative friends, but they were not adding anything meaningful to my life and vice versa. I didn't feel that I could be my true self around them and we always had surface-level conversations. Sometimes it felt forced and almost unnatural to remain connected, but it was done out of some weird sense of obligation that is inexplicable. Those were not true friendships. These friendships are sometimes obtained when you join various social organizations or form friendships with people at work.

Positive friends, on the other hand, are vital to your soul. They won't do things deliberately to hurt you. They tell you the truth but not to harm you but so that you can be a better you. They have your best interests at heart and want to genuinely see you succeed even if it means you are winning more than they are because they know their come up is on the way. They are physically and emotionally available to you and show up for you. They promote you and your business and will help you find that new job so that you can leave the job you hate. Positive friends call to check on you when you are quiet with great concern. They are excited when you get married and do all they can to make sure your wedding is smooth and seamless including getting along with your most challenging family member just so that you can have the best day possible. They're even more excited when you have your first baby, and, later they shout for joy when your child wins the spelling bee and share it on social media as if it were their own. They understand your gifts and remind you that you should be using them. You feel energized when you leave their presence. True friends are not mad at you for things that don't amount to a hill of beans and they certainly don't compete against you instead they get mad at you for all of the right reasons- you lowered your standards for a bum dude that broke your heart.

While you are doing this soul work, it is important that you build a community of positive solid friendships. Healing involves having a safe space to share and vent your feelings without worry. While you are cleansing your soul, you will need people to pour back into you with positivity. As you erase all of the toxicity from your heart and mind — the rejection, the fear, the hurts, the lies, the betrayal, the low self-esteem, the suffering, the belittling, you need friends, a support system, that have wisdom that can build you back up by speaking love and truth into your life. If they do not make healthy decisions for their own lives, they have absolutely no business speaking into yours! True friends, however, will love you, cry with you, celebrate you and pray with you. Healing is done in communities!

It's a challenge for many of us black girls to build a community because some of us have trust issues in terms of dealing with other women. We have been hurt and betrayed by our sisters, so we become guarded. And once the guard is up, it's hard to take it down. We have to forgive and know that there are still good women out there that know how to do friendships. As I have gotten older, I have trimmed down my friend list. Now, I do have many, many associates but I can count on one hand the number of true friendships I have and I'm okay with that. Do you want to know who your true friends are? Think about your last days on this earth, the final minutes before your spirit leaves your body. Who do you see by your side? Who do you see that will be there without question not for the sake of being nosy or to get information to gossip about later with others? Those who would come for the sake of spending one last minute with you. True friendships are those that you know without a doubt will be at your side holding your hand, watching you take your last breath. Those that you know will be there to provide you with any level of comfort they can in your darkest hour are your true friends. Those are the people you need in your community.

If you fill your life with people that think and behave positively, you will do the same. If you saturate yourself with people that have positive things happening to them the same will happen for you. Positivity and negativity are both infectious.

Questions to Journal

Who are the friends that you want by your side when you take your last breath?

Why do you think it's a challenge for you to make and maintain friends?

Do you have any negative friends?

Action Items

Think about ways that you can build a community that includes positive friends.

Think about three positive people in your life that you would like to add to your community. Offer to meet them for coffee.

Anti-Gossip

There is nothing that beats a conversation that includes some good ole juicy gossip — the tea. Sometimes, we bond with other women over gossip. And we love the women that can bring us the tea. Please hear me when I say — we are not our best selves when we gossip. Gossiping requires us to rely on negative thoughts and our unhealed wounds to tear someone down, pick them apart, and focus on the worst parts of them. The more we discuss negative things the more negativity we invite in our lives.

Many times, when people come to us with gossip they are insecure or jealous. Those two spirits (jealousy and insecurity) easily attract others with the same spirits. They know exactly who to come to. People used to come to me with tea often. It was as if they knew I would not only entertain it but enjoy it. I eventually had to ask myself — why do people always come to me with gossip? Did I walk around with a look of misery that was easily identifiable? It forced me to look at myself in the mirror and do some soul searching.

Gossiping is also a very cowardly behavior. It means we do not have the guts to go to that person and say how we feel. Instead, we talk about them behind their back. We have to ask ourselves when we gossip what our desired outcome is — Do we want to get the person we are gossiping with on our side? Do we want to get them to empathize with us? Do we feel that gossiping with another person will help us to build a friendship? Do we feel good because we have shared negative things about another person? If you answered yes to any of these it means it's time to heal. Now when people come to me with gossip I do everything in my power to lift the person they are gossiping about up. I counter every negative thing they have to say with positive things.

Another reason why we gossip is because we have not been taught proper conflict resolution skills. So we gossip hoping that it will magically resolve the problem. Sadly, it doesn't. Often, it makes the situation worse.

The Bible commands us, "though shalt not murder." In this passage, murder is mostly interpreted as physical harm. However, you can murder someone with your tongue as well. Oh, and what a weapon our tongues can be. When we gossip it is akin to murder as we are aiming to kill a person's reputation and spirits. Studies prove that when a person causes physical harm to another person, typically they are filled with a lot of guilt and shame afterward. So, it is with gossip. We cause so much emotional harm to our souls when we gossip that it is just not worth it.

Questions to Journal

What area of your life is filled with the most gossip i.e. family, friends, work, sorority, church?

What causes you to gossip?

Action Items

Try to spend a week without gossip. Increase to a month, then a year.

Heal Through True Love

Owe no man anything, but to love one another, for he that loveth another hath fulfilled the law.

Romans 13:8-10 NIV[1]

From modernized western countries to the most remote and least developed parts of our planet, one experience that we all have shared and desire is love. It was love for people that made Martin Luther King Jr and Mahatma Gandhi take action to change the world. It was love for his wife that made Mughal Emperor Shah Jahan commission the building of the world-renowned Taj Mahal. It was love that made Connecticut teacher, Victoria Soto, risk her life protecting her students during the Sandy Hook shootings. Furthermore, it has been proven that the most common source of depression is feeling unloved. Love gives a person a reason to live! Do you see how powerful love is?

When our Creator reached down from the heavens and formed each of us, He specifically had love in mind. He created us not just to coexist but to be in community with each other. This interdependent relationship that He developed us to have is so that we can enjoy each other while helping each other grow, heal, and learn, all through love. As cliché as it may sound, we were genuinely made to love. I am convinced that we do not live our best lives until we embrace love- love for God, love for self and love for others.

There are many benefits to demonstrating love. When we embrace love, we open up many doors for ourselves, and we are able to gain opportunities that we otherwise would not have access to. Everything we obtain in this life will come through people. If you want to be a great leader, you need solid relationships with the right people to get you there and to help you carry out your vision. If you want to run for office, you need people to support your platform. If you want to write a book, you need people that believe in you and want to hear you out. If you want to run a business, you need people to market the business for you through word of mouth.

Part of the problem is that we do not love God and we do not love ourselves. The Bible commands us to love our neighbor as ourselves. If we do not love ourselves, we can't possibly love others. Quite a few people speak about self-love but do not truly understand what it looks like. Loving yourself shows in your actions: If a person truly loves themselves, they do not spend money irresponsibly. If a person truly loves themselves, they do not abuse harmful illegal substances. If a person truly loves themselves, they do not date bum dudes that mean them no good. If a person loves themselves, they heal so that they can get out of their own way.

The true meaning of love has been lost. Some may feel love means a person spends time with you. That's part of it, but not entirely. Some believe that if someone provides for you or gives you financial support, that is love. Some also believe love means that we must agree on almost everything. That is certainly not love. I've also known women that give their body to men in hopes that love will be returned. I've known men that feel that love can be bought. None of those are true.

We also use the term so loosely. Love has become such a cliché term. We love TV shows, our favorite songs, and movies, but we do not know how to fully love people. In the book *All About Love*, bell hooks argues that we do not have a shared definition of what love truly is. I struggled for a long time to understand how to love. So, I took to the "good book" as my great granny would call it and looked at God, our Creators, definition of love:

In the Bible, I Corinthians 13:1-13[1] gives us several characteristics of true love. When viewing these factors let's look at how we can extend love to others and ourselves.

LOVE IS PATIENT[1]

I find it interesting that the writer, Paul, begins by describing love as patient. It's as if he views patience as one of the most important facets of love. I believe that he wants us to know that when we make a conscious decision to love someone, we must begin with patience. We have become a society that is too quick to stop loving someone because of their flaws.

As an example, I once had a friend that I enjoyed spending girl time with. When she and I linked up I had to hear about her new featured purchase whether it was her new luxury car, her Gucci shades, her Louis Vuitton luggage set, or the pool in her backyard. It annoyed me so I distanced myself from her. Eventually, I realized that I needed to use my self-awareness to ask myself was I doing something to cause her to behave this way when she was with me? What about me made her feel that she needed to brag? Now it's not always our fault but sometimes we need to check to see if a cause and effect relationship is happening.

I also had to realize that my esteem should be as such that her boasting should not impact me. It's my issue if I feel inferior because of her bragging. I also should not feel compelled to match or one-up her bragging. It took me some time, but I realized that her boasting had nothing to do with me but was more so about her need for validation. So, I had to exercise some patience while she evolves. I also needed to be the friend that loves her enough to show her that those things didn't matter and that she has worth that is more valuable than a bag with some rich white guys name on it.

When you genuinely love someone, you are patient with them understanding that they are human and have many flaws just as you do. Being patient means you allow that person to be who they are and love them with their flaws. It does not mean that you accept bad or disrespectful behavior, but you accept their quirks and minor annoyances.

We also need to extend patience to ourselves, this is a huge barrier to fully loving ourselves. We become angry when we make mistakes or feel that we have missed the mark. We are truly our own worst critics. Whenever I give a speech or do any form of public speaking, I critique myself harder than the audience critiques me, "I fidgeted too much, I used too many uhmms, I spoke too slowly or too fast." These are all things I tell myself while the audience is singing my praises and saying what a great job I did. We are human. We need to stop focusing on the mistakes and start embracing the praises.

LOVE IS NOT EASILY ANGERED[1]

As you begin to work on patience, you will find that you are becoming less angry. If you want to see where your unhealed wounds lie, look at what offends you or causes you to become angry. The Bible encourages us to be slow to take offense. When we have patience with others we are not easily angered and less triggered. We realize they are humans and human beings will fail us. That is reality. We must focus on extending grace and forgiveness, especially to the people we love.

LOVE IS KIND[1]

The opposite of love is hate. When a person does not have love in their heart, they react to triggers with hate. Hate manifests itself in acts of unkindness similar to the way love manifests itself in acts of kindness. I can recall dating a man that once did many unkind things to me. It took me a while to realize that he didn't love himself so how could I expect him to love me. You see, when a person doesn't love themselves you can't expect them to love you. His self-hate made him so jaded that everything I did, he perceived it as negative. He had a way of making something so simple appear to be hate-filled. He had been hurt so many times in the past that he completely lacked trust for anyone and felt that everyone was out to get him. Hate changed his perception. He could not see goodness, kindness, or love because hate had taken over and was in full control of him. When we allow love to fill our hearts, we think the best of other people and want to see them win. We do all that we can to help others and will even find ways to lift and encourage others.

We also need to extend kindness to ourselves. This is how we develop self-love. We need to eliminate any negative talk and ideals that do not serve us well emotionally. We need to think only kind and positive thoughts towards ourselves. I teach my daughter to be kind to herself by demonstrating kindness to her. So, I speak to her politely and feed her with affirmations. I also tell her when she is wrong not in a way that makes her feel ashamed or derails her but in such a way that she learns and grows from it. My goal in correcting her is not to harm her but to empower her.

I also spend quality time with my daughter and encourage her to set goals to achieve. I teach her to love and care for her body with all of its flaws helping her to understand that she will only receive one body, so she must listen to it and be kind to it. That level of kindness that I teach my daughter has helped me to develop a healthy love for myself.

When you do not have self-love, you are constantly trying to prove your worth. I can recall a time when I placed my value in material possessions; I felt driving the right car proved that I was valuable. When that didn't work, I earned an MBA and believed that obtaining a powerful position and owning a business would deem me valuable. Any person that I met, the first thing I told them was who I worked for and what I did for a living. I felt that I constantly needed to prove my worth.

It took me a while to get rid of those bad habits and realize that my value is in the fact that I am a strong, capable, black girl and more importantly, a child of the Most High God.

LOVE DOES NOT ENVY[1]

As I discussed previously, when my friends were getting married, I desired to be married as well. Not a bad thing, right? But when the desire consumes us or when we become secretly angry for a person, we have entered into envy and that is an evil emotion. I have seen many friendships end over envy. I have seen marriages dissolve over envy. Envy plagues our history as well. Entire nations have crumbled because of envy, and there has been mass human annihilation due to envy. But the truth is at any time in our life we have and will experience envy. Anyone that tells you they have never experienced envy is straight-up lying to you. We have to use our self-awareness to realize when we have entered an envious space. We need to be quick to check that emotion because it can cause people to do very bad things.

Through all of my husband's successes that often seem to be effortless for him, I have never once experienced envy. I have never once longed to be in his position. That is because I have genuine love for him and love does not envy.

LOVE DOES NOT BOAST OR IS PROUD[1]

There is a quote that states, "the loudest person in the room is the most insecure person in the room." I believe this. Often pride and boasting are tools to hide our insecurities. When we boast or behave in a prideful manner, we are saying look how great I am but look how small you are. Secure people realize they do not have to put others down to be great. If we love someone, we don't want to do things to make them feel small. There is no arrogance in love. God says he hates pride (Prov. 8:13)[1]. You can't serve other people and look out for their best interests when you are focusing and talking about yourself.

In *Mere Christianity*, C.S. Lewis says, "According to Christian teachers, the essential vice, the utmost evil, is pride. unchastity, anger, greed, drunkenness, and all that, are mere fleabites in comparison: it was through pride that the devil became the devil: Pride leads to every other vice: it is the complete anti-God state of mind." I have seen pride destroy marriages, end relationships, and cause murderers. When pride is present, love is lost.

LOVE DOES NOT INSIST ON ITS OWN WAY[1]

Many conflicts consist of two people trying to get each other to see things their way. Think about the last disagreement that you were involved in; what were you trying to accomplish? I'm sure at some point, you were aiming to explain your side and to get the other person to see how they were wrong. That is certainly the sum total of my disagreements. It's perfectly okay to agree to disagree instead of spending energy to prove a point. Love understands that people have opinions and we are not always going to see eye to eye on everything. People will not do things the way we would like. As long as it does not violate our freedoms or causes us harm, give them the freedom to do what pleases them. Love allows people to be who they are.

I have a former boss that I still keep in contact with quite frequently. Once, we had a project that he assigned me to fully manage. As I began to execute, I didn't put a process in place. I simply began to complete the tasks and delegate responsibilities. During the process, I became stressed and overwhelmed, in part, because it became so unorganized. After it was complete, I asked my boss why he did not get involved to help me implement a better process. His response was, "I let you be you. I also needed you to learn, and that would not have happened if I intruded. I became involved when I felt that you really needed me." From that situation, not only did I learn the importance of implementing clear processes, but I learned that love doesn't force it's way.

During a leadership training, TD Jakes stated, "wisdom begins with the notion that I may be wrong[3]." Imagine if we approach every disagreement with the thought that we may be wrong. Instead of focusing on pleading our case - this is something I find myself doing often, for some reason - we should focus on understanding their perspective and hearing their heart. That is how we demonstrate love.

LOVE DOES NOT KEEP RECORD OF WRONGS[1]

Have you ever known someone that keeps a mental file cabinet of all the wrongs that people do to them? They keep that list locked and loaded and ready to use as a weapon. This is another toxic behavior. This is also a behavior that is present in my family. Holding on to wrongs and waiting to use them against someone suffocates relationships and chokes the life out of them. When you hold a grudge, the relationship becomes stagnant right at the place the grudge starts. Love forgives and forgets because we understand that people are human and need grace. Love also understands that we need grace and have been extended grace.

LOVE ALSO DOES NOT DELIGHT IN EVIL BUT REJOICES IN THE TRUTH[1]

We are at a place in our society where we delight ourselves when we hear terrible things about people. There are news outlets, talk shows, and blog sites that earn millions of dollars because people enjoy hearing about the shortcomings of others. It is sad when someone else's pain becomes our entertainment. We discuss it at length, ponder it, and take our stance on it. A healed person does not delight in evil but would rather dwell in their good. People with a heart filled with compassion understand how hard life is and wishes everyone well.

LOVE PROTECTS[1]

Love not only protects physically but it also protects a person's reputation, name, and character. We should not have to tell the world when someone makes a mistake but go to them with love and restore that person. We should be willing to hear them out with a heart of understanding.

If we love ourselves, we should protect our own reputation just the same. We should keep our private lives private and only share our drama with our trusted community. Hopping on social media and exposing our own dirty laundry is not self-love.

LOVE BEARS ALL THINGS, BELIEVES ALL THINGS, HOPES ALL THINGS, ENDURES ALL THINGS[1]

I can only imagine what my grandfather's life would have been like if we had embraced him with love. Of course, we all loved him, but we were hurt and angry with how he hurt our grandmother. We were also angry with my grandmother for her reactions to it. That's a lot of anger for one family to bear.

As a family, we should not have allowed him to be defined by the betrayal. I often imagine what the outcome would have been if we had sat down with him and had conversations about how he felt and what he was experiencing in a healthy way. We should have behaved just as Jesus behaved when they brought to him the woman that was caught in adultery. Do you know what Jesus said when they asked what should be done with the woman? He initially said absolutely nothing. His silence was powerful and still shocks the most competent Biblical scholars to this day. I think Jesus' silence speaks volumes about how we are to handle people that make bad choices. We are to have patience with them and love them in a community. It is hard to love others when we are angry with them or focused on their wrongdoings. Imagine how healed our loved ones would be if we forgave, surrounded them with a community of support, and loved them back to solid emotional health.

My grandfather was the kindest man I have ever known. If you were fortunate enough to have met him, you have a positive story about him. Though we should have dealt with the hurt, the good is what he shall be remembered by.

Questions to Journal

Which of these areas of love do you feel that you struggle in displaying? Why?

Action Items

Write down each of these areas of love as described above. Beside each, list ways that you can demonstrate each. Start with your family, then extend it to friends, then your local community.

Chapter 4
The Black Girl Code

"A man that hath friends must show himself friendly[1]."
Proverbs 18:24.

Let me ask you a question: Have you ever experienced a nervous feeling in the pit of your stomach when you are about to enter a room full of black girls that you don't know? Why do you feel that way? Well, let me explain several reasons for that feeling you experience: For one, you may feel that black girls are often cliquish, and they are not going to let you into their "circle". This causes you to worry that you will spend the event isolated and alone. You may also feel that there is a possibility that you could be ridiculed or rejected for being inappropriately dressed, deemed not fashionable enough, or too flashy. It's the catty reactions of black girls to newbies that we fear the most. Many of us have experienced it and are willing to do anything we can to prevent that from reoccurring. Would you worry as much if you knew that these black girls were going to greet you with open arms the minute you walked through the door? Would you worry as much if you knew that these women were going to embrace you, connect with you, and speak life to you? Or are you the person that scowls when a stranger walks into the room? Are you the person that gives the new girl the once over then rolls your eyes or do you simply ignore her and remain in your clique?

Sis, I have news for you —The person that you reject could be the person that is meant to be your new best friend. The person that you ignore could be the person that promotes your new business or book the hardest. This black girl could also be the one that introduces you to your future husband. They could also be the person that loves you and helps you heal.

A powerful tool that the women in our community lack is a palpable sisterhood, but one specifically for us- a black girl code. The way that we create this black girl code is by making space for our sisters. We should be excited to see another black girl enter the room whether we know her or not or whether she is styled to our standards or not. We need to get to know this sister and invite her into our circles.

In addition, we need to view every single black girl that we meet as our sister. We should view our sisters as a soul with a gift and understand that the gift will shape our lives in some manner. For example, one of my friends is knowledgeable on almost any political or social issue. Our dialogue forces me to look past my own biases and to view things from a wider lens. I also have another friend that supports my endeavors and is always proud of my accomplishments. Having that level of love in my life makes me want to extend the same type of love to others.

I love the scene from the movie *Waiting to Exhale* when the main protagonists Bernadine, Robin, Gloria, and Savannah are having a girl's night in. During this scene, after one too many glasses of champagne, Savannah (played by the late, great Whitney Houston) says "the one man that I love is married with kids." The ladies, tipsy as all get out, giggle and continue to discuss their own frustrations with their men. This scene represents true sisterhood; transparency with no judgment, no ridicule, no side-eyes- just love, support, and laughter. When that type of support is present in your life, regardless of what troubles you experience, you know it's going to be okay because you know you are surrounded by unconditional love, a sisterhood.

Ladies, as we are in the trenches breaking ceilings, destroying generational curses, raising villages, and building legacies, we need a palpable sisterhood to keep us lifted in prayer, love, and support. We need our sisters to mentor us, guide us, laugh, and cry with us as we go through life's journey. It is my sisterhood that has kept me sane, motivated, and helped me to heal.

As we are building the black girl code, we must realize that every sister has a story to tell. She also wants to be loved and accepted. Give her the unconditional love that you want to receive and be open to sharing your story and hearing hers-- without judgment. This level of sharing is how bonds are formed. Greet each sister that you see with a smile recognizing her as your sister and comrade in this malicious race. Give her not just any smile but one that says, "I've got your back." You never know what is on her mind or in her path. Perhaps she is nervous because she is headed into a job interview, or maybe she got fired from her job, perhaps she just had a fight with her lover, or perhaps she is uncertain of her future. In a world where the odds are against us, knowing that you are supported by a force is key and that smile will let her know that.

Also, we need to be willing to help each other without looking for anything in return. Can I be honest? There are times when I despise asking another sister for help of any sort. Why? Because past experience has taught me that I will not get it. There are other ways to help someone aside from providing financial means. We need to be willing to help each other by mentoring, sharing professional resources, promoting, providing guidance, or a listening ear. It takes nothing away from us, except a little time, to help someone. In fact, it's good karma. If you help someone, there is someone out there that will help you when you need it and we all need help from time to time.

I want to leave you with this final thought: We have often heard it said that women are emotional beings. Sometimes that is used to demean us or to belittle our abilities to lead or to possess any measure of power. It has been used to portray us as weak and that we do not have the mental fortitude to push past our emotions to consider the facts. Regardless, the fact remains that our body produces more hormones and that causes emotions. But we have to learn to embrace this as a positive thing. Our emotions are truly jewels that we carry that allow us to be nurturers. They equip us with laser keen instincts that allow us to perceive when trouble lies ahead, and they also make us more people-intelligent in that we can sense the feelings of others. Because of our emotions, we are also better communicators — and in my opinion, all of this makes us supreme human beings. We need to learn to tap into these powerful emotions to nurture each other back to solid emotional well- being. As queen mothers, aunties, godmothers, and future matriarchs, we need to use these powerful emotions to end the generational trauma that destroys our families. We have to decide to unite as a community of sisters to heal ourselves and each other using love as our guide.

Now that you are at the end of this book, this will not be the last time that you feel offended or offend someone else. What will be different is the way in which you process it which is where the freedom lies. As we focus on healing our wounds, we will show up as beings filled with love and compassion and, instead of being tolerated, we will be embraced just like a good batch of potato salad at a summer barbecue.

As black girls, our history is difficult and complex. But what was designed to destroy us made us much more powerful. You see, our white sisters were born into privilege, far more than we had. They were amongst the majority and were entitled to privileges that we could only dream about at one time. When you are born into privilege you are expected to succeed because the odds are in your favor and you are equipped with all of the tools and resources for success. But as for black girls, we were not graced with those benefits. We come from a lineage filled with darkness whereas we once were queens in our own land, we were then enslaved becoming concubines, mammies, nannies, and single mothers. The odds were stacked high against us. However, we have overcome that dark history to become mothers, professionals, artists, entrepreneurs, influencers, thinkers and more importantly -emotionally whole. Now that's real black girl magic.

Action Items

List 3 behavioral changes you will implement that you learned from reading this book.

Purpose to be more open to black girls. Greet them with a smile when you see them.

Appendix: Establishing Identity

As we have discussed, for many of us, our identities were not established early on in our development. Some of the battles that we face in our relationships are reflections of our lack of self-confidence; we need to have confidence in our self and a firm understanding of who we are in order to maneuver successfully in life. As you are deprogramming bad habits and rebuilding your thinking, I want to encourage you to meditate and internalize the following scriptures. These are necessary to help establish a stable identify and build you inner confidence:

Sis, you are beautiful!
I praise you because I am fearfully and wonderfully made; your works are wonderful, I know that full well.
—Psalm 139:14

You are child of God. That is powerful!
Yet to all who did receive him, to those who believed in his name, he gave the right to become children of God.
— John 1:12

God knew you and your circumstances before you were born.
Before I formed you in the womb I knew you, before you were born I set you apart.
— Jeremiah 1:5

God has chosen you!
But you are a chosen people, a royal priesthood, a holy nation, God's special possession, that you may declare the praises of him who called you out of darkness into his wonderful light.
— 1 Peter 2:9

If your earthly parents were unable to care for you, your heavenly father stepped in on their behalf. If you are reading this, that means you are still here. It may not have been easy, but God has been with you and it was all for a greater purpose.
Though my father and mother forsake me, the LORD will receive me.
— Psalm 27:10

Focus on God and He will provide you with peace.
You will keep in perfect peace those whose minds are steadfast, because they trust in you.
— Isaiah 26:3

If you make God first in your life, He will provide and take care for you. He wants your heart!
Look at the birds of the air; they do not sow or reap or store away in barns, and yet your heavenly Father feeds them. Are you not much more valuable than they? Can any one of you by worrying add a single hour to your life?
— Matthew 6:26-34

Girl talk to God. He hears you and will answer.
I sought the LORD, and he answered me; he delivered me
from all my fears.
—Psalm 34:4

Notes

Introduction

1. https://dictionary.cambridge.org/us/dictionary/english/triggered
2. 7 June 2017 https://iwpr.org/publications/status-black-women-united-states-report/
3. 8 July 2015 https://www.psychologytoday.com/us/blog/wander-woman/201507/5-steps-managing-your-emotional-triggers
4. 2017 https://centerforanxietydisorders.com/what-is-trauma/
5. 13 Mar. 2013 https://www.psychologytoday.com/us/blog/workings-well-being/201703/how-heal-the-traumatized-brain

Chapter 1 How did We Get Here

Generational Trauma

1. Beras, Erika. "Traces of Genetic Trauma Can be Tweaked." 15 April 2017 https://www.scientificamerican.com/podcast/episode/traces-of-genetic-trauma-can-be-tweaked
2. Wright, Bright. 1971. Clean Up Woman. *I Love the Way You Love*, Alsten, 1971. album
3. Salt-N-Pepa. 1986. I'll Take Your Man. *Hot, Cool, and Vicious,* Next Plateau Records Inc., 1986. CD
4. Brandy and Monica. 1998. The Boy is Mine. *Never Say Never,* Darkchild, 1998. CD
5. Cardi B. 2018. Money. *Money,* J White Did It, 2018. CD

Mommy Issues

1. Jakes, TD, *Effective Leadership*, New Year's Joint Revival, Jan. 2006. Upper Marlboro, MD
2. 7 Feb 2020 https://www.encyclopedia.com/people/history/historians-miscellaneous-biographies/td-jakes
3. *Friday*. Directed by F Gary Gray, New Line Productions, 1995.

Daddy Issues

1. *The Holy Bible*, New International Version (2000). Cincinnati, OH: New International Version
2. 2018 http://fathers.com/statistics-and-research/the-extent-of-fatherlessness/
3. Sweeton, Jennifer. "The Three Parts of your Brain that Can be Affected by Trauma." 8 Jul 2018 https://psychcentral.com/blog/the-3-parts-of-your-brain-affected-by-trauma/
4. *The Holy Bible*, New International Version (2000). Cincinnati, OH: New International Version

Bullying

1. *Friday*. Directed by F Gary Gray, New Line Productions, 1995.
2. *The Holy Bible*, New International Version (2000). Cincinnati, OH: New International Version

The Devil

1. *The Holy Bible*, New International Version (2000). Cincinnati, OH: New International Version

Chapter 2 the Healing Process

Contentment

1. https://www.dictionary.com/browse/discontent
2. *The Holy Bible*, New International Version (2000). Cincinnati, OH: New International Version

Chapter 3 Soul Cleansing

1. *The Holy Bible*, New International Version (2000). Cincinnati, OH: New International Version

Heal Through Love

1. *The Holy Bible*, New International Version (2000). Cincinnati, OH: New International Version
2. Lewis, C.S., *Mere Christianity,* 1952
3. Jakes, TD, *Leadership Training*, New Year's Revival, Jan. 2020. Upper Marlboro, MD
4. Hooks, Bell, *All About* Love: New Visions, (2000)

All scriptures are from the New International Version of the Holy Bible

Made in the USA
Monee, IL
29 November 2020